D0780559

REFRAMING DIVERSITY IN EDUCATION

HOW TO ORDER THIS BOOK

BY PHONE: 800-233-9936 or 717-291-5609, 8AM–5PM Eastern Time

BY FAX: 717-295-4538

BY MAIL: Order Department
Technomic Publishing Company, Inc.
851 New Holland Avenue, Box 3535
Lancaster, PA 17604, U.S.A.

BY CREDIT CARD: American Express, VISA, MasterCard

EDUCATIONAL LEADERSHIP FOR THE 21ST CENTURY

REFRAMING DIVERSITY IN EDUCATION

Joan Poliner Shapiro, Ed.D.

Associate Dean
Department of Educational Leadership and Policy Studies
College of Education, Temple University

Trevor E. Sewell, Ph.D.

Dean, Department of Psychological Studies
College of Education, Temple University

Joseph P. DuCette, Ph.D.

Associate Dean, Department of Psychological Studies
College of Education, Temple University

SERIES EDITOR: WILLIAM J. BAILEY

LANCASTER · BASEL

Reframing Diversity in Education
a **TECHNOMIC**® publication

Published in the Western Hemisphere by
Technomic Publishing Company, Inc.
851 New Holland Avenue, Box 3535
Lancaster, Pennsylvania 17604 U.S.A.

Distributed in the Rest of the World by
Technomic Publishing AG
Missionsstrasse 44
CH-4055 Basel, Switzerland

Printed in the United States of America
10 9 8 7 6 5 4 3 2 1

Main entry under title:
Educational Leadership for the 21st Century – Reframing Diversity in Education

A Technomic Publishing Company book
Bibliography: p. 133
Includes index p. 153

Library of Congress Catalog Card No. 94-62046
ISBN No. 1-56676-240-5

To our parents whose stories have helped to shape both our personal and professional lives. We thank and honor Ruth and Isadore Poliner, Nerissa and Vincent Sewell, and Dorothy and Joseph DuCette.

CONTENTS

PREFACE TO THE SERIES

ANY ADULT, WITH even a small awareness of public affairs, living in the last decade of the 20th century knows two things about public education. First, a quality education is absolutely essential to individuals in a democracy facing the rapid changes of the future. Second, the present public education system has lost credibility with the majority of taxpayers. Interestingly enough, a recent survey shows that most parents think public schools are not doing their job, but that "their school" is satisfactory. Clearly, the advent of educational reform literature in the 1980s and 1990s offers many solutions; however, even more clearly, the public schools are very slow and reluctant to change. The theories offered on educational reform illustrate the problem—a large discrepancy between what is possible and what is common practice.

Short of rewriting the federal Constitution regarding the responsibilities of the states to provide for a free and public educational system, the American public schools need a total revamping of structure, philosophy, pedagogy, and professionalism. This professional educator's library is designed to explain why significant changes are needed and how changes can be made given the present constitutional authority.

How is this library different than the other polemics of reform? The literature is replete with articles, books, technical reports, national studies, state reviews, and speeches—not the least of which comes from politicians. The literature covers structure, instruction, curriculum, support services, and educational leadership; however, most of the topics in these documents are unrelated. Busy administrators and harassed teachers cannot pull all of this disparate advice together for total, quality, and comprehensive change. This book series library takes the basic components of an educational system and, in a coordinated manner, delineates how system reform can work.

Each author, an expert in his/her respective field, addresses three pertinent themes wrought from many hours of research and discussion: increased professionalism, accountability, and technology. Additionally, each author presents future oriented practices germane to their field. Our overriding vision is to develop scholarly practitioners for the 21st century, who demonstrate deliberative responses to the cultural demands placed on education.

WILLIAM J. BAILEY
Series Editor

PREFACE

AMERICA HAS ALWAYS been a country composed of diverse groups from diverse cultures. We were founded on the philosophical principle that *all* people were created equal (although the founding fathers were a bit more restrictive in their use of language) and that all people were born with inalienable rights. Presumably, among these rights was the possibility of an equal chance for a quality education, regardless of race, gender, social class, physical disability, or a host of other conditions.

Yet the history of our attempts to educate all of the people in the country demonstrates the opposite. We have not, broadly as a nation, or narrowly as the providers of education for our children, been willing or able to use and value the diversity that exists in our schools. Partly, this is because we have, for too long and under too many circumstances, allowed racism and sexism to dominate our thinking. Partly, it is because we have adhered aggressively to a philosophy of science that seeks to find the one best method to solve a problem. But whether by fault or by philosophy, we have created schools that too often require conformity to a single approach, that establish standards and use assessment techniques that favor one group over another, and that do not allow students to use their individual strengths.

It is clear that the time is long overdue for this to change. As a nation, we are becoming increasingly diverse. It is estimated that by the year 2000, at least four states will have populations in which whites will be in the minority. Even if this weren't true, there is still great diversity even among the white, male, middle-class population which has dominated American education for over 200 years. Unfortunately these aspects of diversity (e.g., differences in learning style, differences in cognitive ability, differences in physical ability, etc.) have typically been ignored and/or belittled. Diversity should have always been the basis for educational practices; it is now becoming evident that we can waste no more time in moving in this direction.

Our purpose in writing this book is to review the general area of student diversity and the way that these variables affect a student's ability to learn. We believe that the topics included in this book, although not exhaustive, are representative of the current thinking in this field. In many cases, we have included references and resources where the reader may find additional and more in-depth presentations. Our hope is that our coverage will lead interested readers to pursue these additional resources.

Parts of this book have been published by Jossey-Bass in the American Association of Colleges of Teacher Education's (AACTE) *A Knowledge Base for Teacher Educators* (1995) edited by Frank Murray. In particular, Chapters 3 and 5 are similar to our presentation in the AACTE volume. In addition, Chapters 2 and 4 contain material that is somewhat similar to the earlier presentation, although both have been expanded. Chapters 1, 6, and 7 are completely new for this book. We are deeply thankful for the AACTE's permission to include these sections in the present book.

UNDERSTANDING "SELF"

> . . . people must first understand themselves before they can hope to understand others. (Sleeter and Grant, 1988, p. 126)

AT THE OUTSET, we want to explicitly recognize that the area of diversity is complex, confusing, and sometimes emotional. This hit home to us, as a writing team, as we attempted to find a common ground to begin this book. In our discussions of diversity, we realized that it was important to speak about who we are as educators and as people, before moving on to the various categories of diversity.

We have begun to realize that who we are greatly affects our thinking about categories such as ethnicity, social class, gender, and other areas of difference. Through our explorations and discussions during the process of writing this book, we have had to grapple with who we are and start from an awareness of what makes each of us different and also what makes us similar. This self-analysis, we believe, has acted as a stepping stone enabling us to turn to other categories of difference, that may not have impacted on us directly, with empathy and a willingness to understand and grow.

Viewing the three of us in aspects of difference, in somewhat of a superficial way, not only do we come from different academic disciplines, but we are also different along several other critical dimensions. From the perspective of diversity, each of us could be described succinctly in the following ways:

- a white, Jewish, northeastern, middle-class, heterosexual, middle-aged, English-speaking female
- an African-American, Protestant, mid-Atlantic, middle-class, heterosexual, middle-aged, English-speaking male

- a white, Catholic, midwestern, middle-class, heterosexual, middle-aged, English-speaking male

What became clear to us, in generating the above list, is that even these adjectives do not begin to fully describe the ways that we are different. These descriptors, for example, do not mention that one of us has had considerable background in the area of race, whereas another has written about gender. They also do not indicate our approach to educational research. One of us has been trained and continues to work in the positivistic tradition; another is comfortable crossing the paradigms from the positivistic to the interpretive paradigm; whereas the other is much more at home following the naturalistic or interpretive tradition.

Although our training and approaches to research are important, we realized that they do not describe us in enough detail to indicate who we are and how we differ from each other. During our working luncheons, with the development of trust, we began to speak of our backgrounds and those critical incidents that shaped us. In fact, we discovered that each of us had stories to tell about our past that in many ways set the stage for our professional lives as educators.

We would like to briefly share with you a little of our background and a few critical incidents, relating to diversity, that helped to form our current views on diversity in education. We hope that you will read these stories not just as the isolated experiences of three unique educators, but rather as models for your own reflections. Such reflections may be useful before embarking on the study of one or more of the areas of diversity that are familiar to you. Once involved in the literature in a particular category, such as social class, the hope would be that you would want to study other categories that may relate to your life less directly or may relate to those you work with or teach.

THREE AUTOBIOGRAPHIES

Joan's Story

My mother says that I have a selective memory, and she is right. Nevertheless, what I have chosen to highlight in this story are salient memories and critical incidences, relating to a few categories of diversity, that helped to shape me as a person and as a professional. In particular, when I take the time to reflect, there is one category of difference that developed over time into a major focus in my life—that category was gender—but it took its time to truly take hold. Along with gender, throughout my life, different forms of diversity surfaced and collectively left their marks on me.

Awareness of my ethnic background as a Jew came early as I was born and raised in Connecticut, in a tiny city composed primarily of Americans from Italian descent. The local citizens modified the pronunciation of my family's last name to make it sound Italian and familiar. My family accepted the change in pronunciation agreeably because it enabled us to pass and feel more comfortable within the community. Nevertheless, in a city of predominately Italian-American Catholics, I felt different from others, particularly on religious holidays and when I attended Hebrew school.

When I reflect about those early years, it is clear to me that gender issues were just below the surface. However, raised as I was with a male cousin my own age, there was little I felt I could not do. My cousin and I tended to both cooperate and compete in most arenas, and I often felt like "one of the boys." However, it took a critical incident at the end of my junior year of high school, at a time when my rank was second in the class, to end this illusion. One day a boy approached me and said in something of a prophetic tone, "You'll take chemistry next year. Girls don't do well in chemistry. You'll see." Whether it was a self-fulfilling prophecy or a willingness on my part to accept a stereotype or a hex of some kind, his prediction came true. Ultimately, in my stead, he graduated as Salutatorian while I looked on, accepting my place in the class with goodwill.

I wish that I could tell you that my postsecondary education at a woman's college in Boston made a great difference to me and led to genuine consciousness-raising, but this was not the case. I imagine that I was not ready, nor, to be fair, was most of society. Although my college did expose me to some outstanding women professors; nevertheless, in the early 1960s, the majority of the faculty and the administration of the college were still predominately men. I was also constrained by the limited range of career options offered mainly within the boundaries of traditional female professions. But Boston itself was exciting and served as a center for civil rights protests. Like others of my generation, I was deeply affected by this movement and came to regard protests as almost a civic responsibility. The crowning protest for me came after graduation, during my honeymoon, when my new British husband, my brother-in-law, and I spent a memorable afternoon as the only whites attending a Martin Luther King address in Washington, D.C. As a Jew, I felt considerable empathy with African-Americans and was deeply moved when we sang together, "We Shall Overcome."

Along with race and ethnicity, social class, as a category, made an impact. This initially occurred when I taught British history to secondary school female students in London, England, in the mid-1960s. My students had not passed the 11 + Exam and were relegated to a secondary modern school with little chance for higher education. My students were on the whole intelligent; and yet many had not received the advantages of a middle-class upbringing. The best that these young women could hope to attain were blue-collar jobs working on the nearby high street. While I was teaching in England, the Labor government mandated comprehensive education and my local school merged with the nearby college preparatory grammar school. At long last, I thought, my students would have some opportunity. But I was wrong. In the new comprehensive high school, tracking or "streaming," as the British called it, appeared on the scene. Thus, the status quo remained as students from the working class continued to be sorted, categorized, and kept in their place within English society.

Thus far in my life, my consciousness had been raised in a number of categories of difference, but it took a critical incident for me to focus with more awareness on the area of diversity that I would be studying for years to come. It was Uncle Max's funeral that was the turning point for me in the category of gender. Uncle Max's funeral took place in the Northern part of England, in which a very fundamentalist sect of Jews dwelled. When my husband and I arrived at Uncle Max's home, the women were moaning and wailing around a hearse that waited outside the door. This seemed strange to me as Uncle Max was well into his eighties and had not suffered unduly before his death. I went to the burial ground for the ceremony with my husband. At the grounds, much to my surprise, I turned out to be the only woman present and was told not to leave the car. Apparently, women were not allowed on the burial grounds lest they sully the soil. This was a painful experience for me as I had only recently buried my father, in the conservative Jewish tradition, and my mother, sister, daughter and I had been free to mourn in public and on the cemetery grounds. It seemed to me that the humiliation for women continued that day when the Rabbi told Auntie Minnie, Uncle Max's wife of forty-five years, that she missed an excellent speech he had given on behalf of her husband on the burial grounds. All the women around me seemed to accept what I perceived to be an insult without comment, but I was never the same. The category of gender emerged as the most salient aspect of diversity in my life.

After Uncle Max's funeral, it became clear to me that there was much I needed to know about women. I began to read and learn about women and their lives. I also had to deal soon with the realities of motherhood and the decision to stay at home or continue working. Most of the women in my family knew their place. They remained at home as full-time mothers and there was little encouragement to maintain a professional life. It was difficult for me to leave my baby daughter, Suzie, while I supervised intern teachers. But I felt it was important to do so despite the constant feelings of guilt. Many women of my generation have had to face these conflicts and constraints. However, in my case, involvement in the field of women's studies provided sanity, offering me explanations outside of self-blame for the difficulties and conflicts I faced. Learning about power, privilege, and patriarchy helped empower me to attempt to begin to solve some of my dilemmas and deal with society. However, although less frequently now, I find myself doubting and sliding back, allowing the system to put me once again in my place. Then it is that I hear the words, "girls don't do well in chemistry" and, this time, they challenge me to go on and prove him wrong. Thus, I have tried to persevere, speaking out and writing about gender issues and doing my best to translate the voices of women of all colors as well as the voices of others so that those in power may hear, understand, and grow.

Trevor's Story

To write my story in the context of appreciating or understanding diversity generates extreme emotional conflicts. The experiences that shape my views on diversity and other educational issues are marked by pride in personal accomplishments that are enmeshed in the highly controlled rage of a black person and the deepening agony of class conflicts.

I was born in Jamaica and grew up under colonial rule. The country gained independence two months before my twenty-second birthday, and I left Jamaica to study in America two months after that birthday. This is a salient historical fact because any introspective look at myself and educational thoughts must be examined in the context of the radical psychological shift from my self-perceptions as a youth in Jamaica to that of a black American. Despite the misery of poverty, the striking lack of educational opportunities and humiliating oppressive social forces, I grew up thinking of myself as an individual with many desirable personal attributes. I didn't for a moment think of myself as a black person with any of the stereotypical attributes with which I was later and currently judged.

I grew up interacting with bright, talented, and ambitious youngsters who could not aspire to enter high school because their parents, like mine, couldn't pay for the educational privileges afforded only the affluent in the society. I grew up under conditions in which many individuals could have been, but were not, engulfed in a tangle of despair created by the lack of opportunities to support their ambition. I grew up under conditions in which many internalized the belief that one's destiny was determined by ability, effort, or personal integrity but was limited by socioeconomic circumstances. Nevertheless, from a personal perspective, there was no evidence to suggest that these experiences or perceptions produced psychological despair, hopelessness, or shattered dreams to the extent that they created a limitation on one's motivation to strive for success.

The pervasive reality of poverty was widely interpreted as a historical accident rooted in social-class interests rather than racial conflicts. Thus, poverty was not usually perceived as an insurmountable barrier to academic, social, and economic success. For one to be caught in the entrapment of limited and often debilitating options as a result of poverty was not unusual. But to interpret one's existential plight as if one were caught in a psychological web of helplessness was quite unusual.

Perhaps the most significant childhood phrase that I recall was the passionate words of my mother—"poverty is not a disgrace." And because I vehemently disagreed with this perspective, she tried to condition me to believe that poverty by itself will not destroy one's self-respect, dignity, aspirations, and hope. Relentlessly, my parents emphasized the virtues of hard work, honesty, and good manners, the latter of which was a top priority. Respect for others, they thought, was a fundamental prerequisite for a good life. They maintained that if one practices these virtues, social mobility is possible regardless of the socioeconomic circumstances in which one was born.

Recognizing the great chasm in the social-class structure in a colonized country in which the population was overwhelmingly black, my mother implicitly transmitted hope despite the formidable barriers to educational equity and economic opportunities. Like most children at the time, I was allowed to dream of greatness and to think of myself as being special with the potential for great accomplishments if the opportunity arose. In my world, at an early age, humiliating encounters with the "haves" or the privileged individuals of the society were taken in the spirit that eventually one could achieve highly coveted positions and status. Wherever self-hatred, the lack of motivation, and failure were evident; they were not attributed to the ravages of racism. Looking back, I must assume that racism was brilliantly masked under the cloak of the acceptable social-class structure of the society.

As a proud and confident young man, I arrived in America relatively naive about who I was as a black person. Within days of my arrival in Wisconsin, I was forced to make a dramatic shift from my self-perception of simply being another individual human being, to thinking of myself first as a black man. Social class was no longer the preeminent factor in the concerns now being considered under issues of diversity—race became the all-important variable. Even though my academic performance was consistently impressive, my confidence gradually eroded and dreams of greatness became struggles of how to avoid frequent humiliating experiences associated with racial stereotypic assumptions of ability and other unflattering personality attributes.

In one year I read more black literature than I had read in my earlier twenty-two years of life. I was particularly interested in understanding how great African-Americans succeeded against such extraordinary odds. I was interested in knowing how black children perform academically, establish socially desirable goals, and strive to achieve greatness as Americans in the face of, what was for me, traumatizing despair.

I pondered the psychological effects of being labeled intellectually inferior merely by racial characteristics. I analyzed the revolting experience of being told, "we don't serve your kind," and I desperately sought psychological relief in outstanding academic performance, but there was no escape. As I struggled to maintain my humanity in the face of the most disrespectful and degrading experiences, I observed the behavior of white men and women who truly embraced diversity and offered moral support to students regardless of their ethnic, racial, or social-class background. These individuals valued diversity before the passage of the civil rights legislative actions because they recognized that no one group of people has a monopoly on academic excellence, talent, or giftedness. Their actions offered comforting optimism even in the scorching depths of despair that perhaps subsequent generations will inherit an enduring legacy of racial harmony.

Given my personal encounters with issues of social class and race, my preoccupation with poverty, motivation, intellectual assessment, and intelligence testing of minority students as research interests can be of no great surprise. If the opportunity to learn is relatively obscure and restrictive; if racial conflict, real or perceived, haunts one's self-esteem; and if everyday experiences validate the historical constraints and visions of achievements, what strategies will instill pride and foster academic engagement in educational settings in which diversity must be recognized and valued?

Issues of diversity, for me, are always framed within the racial context that during my lifetime America will not choose to accept me with the same dignity and respect accorded to others, regardless of my personal accomplishments or legal or legislative safeguards. Because of America's enduring problem of racism, I am deeply convinced that as African-Americans, we will first be judged by our color rather than by any social class distinction. Yet, issues of diversity and multiculturalism must be debated from the perspective that no American, regardless of ethnicity, gender, disability, sexual orientation, social class, or race is born branded for failure.

Joe's Story

Without a very deep analysis, it should be evident that I am the nondiverse member of the diverse team that is writing this book: the white, middle-class male. In fact, the differences between my background and the backgrounds of my two coauthors are even deeper than appear on the surface.

I was born in a small city in Wisconsin about 100 miles from Minneapolis, Minnesota (think of it as Lake Wobegone's sister city). In my hometown when I was growing up, there were no African-Americans (a term we would not have used or even understood), no Asians, and no Hispanics. As far as I knew there were no Jews, or if there were they remained silent and unobtrusive. There were no homeless. Although there was a large group of Native Americans (again, a term we would neither have used nor understood) who lived less than thirty miles away and who, in time, would become politically active and would successfully sue the federal government for control of the county in which they lived, they were also essentially silent and invisible. In a time before mainstreaming, there were no children who were explicitly labeled as "retarded" or "learning disabled": the education of retarded children being handled in an institution fifteen miles away in the country; learning disability being a condition which did not, as yet, exist as a recognizable syndrome. There were, as far as I knew, only two major factors that differentiated people: if you were Catholic or Protestant; and if your ancestors came from Sweden or from somewhere else.

It would be incorrect to assume that any of this occurred to me at the time. Like my family and my friends, I was raceless and classless; I was American. Moreover, I do not have much of a sense of being aware of gender, at least as a dominant issue in the way anyone was treated or the expectations that were applied to anybody about what they could do or who they could become. Not that these expectations didn't exist or that they didn't profoundly affect most of the females with whom I went to school; I was simply unaware of them. In the parochial schools, which I attended through high school, male and female roles were firmly and unquestionably described and accepted. When I looked in the mirror I saw a person. I assumed that everyone else saw exactly the same thing.

My undergraduate education was obtained from the branch campus of the University of Wisconsin located in my hometown. There were no people of color that I can remember on the faculty and almost none among the student body. I left in 1964 to go to graduate school at Cornell. Cornell, of course, was very different from where I had spent the first twenty-one years of my life, at least in terms of its student body. The faculty of the psychology department, however, where I obtained my Ph.D., contained twenty-two white males and one white female. The one female left after my second year.

It should be obvious that none of this background prepared me for the life I found in Philadelphia when I arrived in 1968. Philadelphia was then, as now, a multicultural, multiracial city where issues of social class and race and ethnicity were inescapable. I can think of no single event that suddenly made me aware of how insular my life had been. Rather, there were a series of incidents almost too numerous to mention: the times when I was the only white person on the bus; the discussion groups where I was the only non-Jewish member; the countless people who assumed that anyone from a small town in Wisconsin would understand a lot about cows and little about anything else; the many talks with students and peers who had strong ethnic identities and with whom I seemed to share no common basis for communication. In sum, the many times when I was the "other" and everyone else seemed to possess a shared identity that set me apart and made me different.

For me, and for many Americans who were born and raised in the numerous bastions of sameness that characterize large parts of the North American continent, the lessons of diversity are learned with difficulty and often with reluctance. Yet these lessons are critical for several reasons. First, diversity is an inescapable fact of what we currently are as a nation and what we increasingly will become. Those who live in places like Philadelphia do not need to be convinced of this. But even in small towns in Wisconsin the times have already changed: the Hmong people who were relocated there after the Vietnam War; the increasing numbers of African-Americans who have moved there to work in the computer industry; the Menominee Indians who will no longer remain silent; the disabled boy who sits next to my nephew in his seventh grade classroom—all represent aspects of diversity that can neither be ignored nor denied.

It is striking to me that the Wisconsin to which Trevor moved when he left Jamaica is not the same Wisconsin that I left when I went to Cornell, even though both events occurred at almost exactly the same time. The issue is not simply that we create our own reality, for such a point hardly needs to be made in this postmodern era. Rather, the critical question is how we escape our reality to allow the existence of other realities and other perspectives. As the white, middle-class male in this writing team, it is easy to see how this question has special salience for me. As I have indicated above, the realization that I was something other than a person was more difficult for me than for either Joan or Trevor. I assume I share this characteristic with many other white, middle-class males, and it is understandable why so many presentations of diversity begin by focusing on my group.

And yet, even this is probably too simple a lesson. The acceptance and understanding of difference is an issue for everyone, and I suspect that each of us must resolve how we will navigate the difficult waters between self and others. As a product of the 1960s, I am often appalled by the separatism and negativism of these times, and I find it hard to accept the desire on the part of African-Americans, Hasidic Jews, or Italian-Americans to want their own schools and their own curriculum so that they can develop and maintain their own identity. Perhaps this is difficult for me because in always having an identity (or in never realizing that I needed one), none of these issues have been particularly salient in my life. Perhaps the main lesson that I have learned from the experience of writing this book is that issues of identity should be important to all people of color, even if that color is white.

THE LESSONS OF DIVERSITY

We have presented these autobiographies to demonstrate our own journeys into the area of diversity. In view of our differences, we have had some difficult dialogues in attempting to define and discuss diversity. In many ways, we came to issues from our own backgrounds regarding aspects of diversity and from readings we embarked upon that were related to the separate categories of difference that we felt to be most meaningful to each of us.

Not only have our own stories and readings impacted on how we see the world, but our formal educational preparation and the disciplines we were trained in have done so as well. What we have come to realize in our discussions is that we frame questions in different ways, and we base our questions on different knowledge bases and on different ways of knowing. For example, one of us is likely to ask questions that focus on the characteristics that an individual student brings to a situation affecting that individual's success in school and in life. Another would more likely look at the context and/or the group to help determine a student's success or failure within the school or society. At a deeper and more philosophical level, we also began to realize that our definitions of success in both school and life were very different. We discovered that our personal and professional ethical codes were not the same. In fact, there was a point at which we wondered if this diverse writing team could meet the challenge of writing about diversity at all.

The fact that this book was finally completed was based on two realizations: 1) only when we became aware of our own diversity and in the way that our backgrounds, attitudes, and training affected the way we framed educational questions and the answers we sought, were we able to write the book; and 2) our diversity, which initially was a disadvantage, became in the final analysis the critical factor that made the finished product possible. We now have come to believe that anyone of us, alone, would have been incapable of completing the book.

Paradoxically, our commonalities began to appear as the writing process unfolded. Often through compromise and sometimes miraculously through consensus, we were able to not only deal with but also appreciate differences of background, training, and opinion and begin to speak with one voice. The lesson to us, therefore, is that diversity can be a problem if it is allowed to be so, but it can create unforeseen possibilities if accepted and studied. Diversity provides a starting point enabling us to move beyond the categories of difference we have experienced towards other uncharted areas, sometimes leading to commonalities and complex insights. Through the reflection of our own backgrounds and with critical incidences revealed, it is our belief that we were then ready to explore others' stories, empathize with other peoples' experiences, and seek new knowledge about difference. We hope that other educators will attempt this self-reflective process and ultimately feel better prepared to move on to understandings beyond "self" towards varied categories of diversity and towards the understanding of others.

AUTOBIOGRAPHY AND DIVERSITY

We begin this book with our autobiographies because we believe the process that we have undergone might be instructive for others who are in similar positions. It seems to us that many of the books and articles on diversity portray both experienced and new teachers and experienced and new administrators as parochial and unable to understand others. Although we believe that this is not so, it is true that the entire area of diversity can be overwhelming if the goal is to fully understand every student, teacher, and administrator in any specific school. As teacher educators, we have had to ask ourselves how to adequately prepare our preservice teachers for the vast diversity that they will encounter in their careers. It is conceivable that an adequate job could be done if we were to focus on one aspect of diversity (e.g., race) and then to narrow this down even further to focus on one specific group (e.g., African-Americans). Although this might prepare our students for teaching African-American students, it would leave them unprepared to teach Asians or Hispanics. Taken to its logical conclusion, the emphasis on diversity makes it clear that we can never acquire a knowledge base that covers every possible aspect of difference.

We are also aware that the area of multicultural education (which, for us, is a critical, although partial, component of diversity) is often criticized for its emphasis on the three "F's": food, festivals, and fun. While none of these are inappropriate as aspects of a course on multicultural education, they do not constitute a curriculum for diversity. As we said above, a complete curriculum for diversity is logically impossible. We are offering instead a focus on self-awareness through autobiography as a critical starting point. Through self-awareness, we believe that female teachers can be empowered and in turn they can empower others. Through autobiography, male administrators can begin to understand who they are, what their educational beliefs are, where their beliefs come from, and additionally, but most importantly, how they are perceived in schools and in society by other groups. Thus, during their administrative and teacher preparation, through the use of autobiography and self-reflection, future educators will have the opportunity to take part in important conversations about issues of empowerment, power, privilege, and positionality and how these concepts relate to them as teachers and administrators and as human beings.

Autobiography is not new in the field of education. Over the years, a number of interesting autobiographies have emerged. Autobiographies of educators have become best-sellers and in some instances, have created heroes and heroines. Among them are the writings of Pat Conroy (1972), Nathalie Gehrke (1987), Herbert Kohl (1984), Sarah Lawrence Lightfoot (1988), Sylvia Ashton Warner (1963), and many others. Not only are individual names included under the category of autobiography, but group stories, such as the first year teaching tales written by the new teachers, in the book by Ryan (1970) entitled, *Don't Smile Until Christmas,* have also found their place in the literature of schooling. Classroom teachers as well as educators in general are telling their stories, as in the case of the reflections of thirty-three distinguished educators (Burleson, 1991). Recently, because of the emphasis on ethnographic research, action research, and the teacher as researcher, a new group of stories has emerged—some as biographies and others in the form of action research projects. Among them are the stories of African-American female teachers as told to Foster (1991) and the research projects carried out by teachers and reported in books edited by Cochran-Smith and Lytle (1994) and Goswami and Stillman (1987). Additionally, teachers have worked through their own feelings and knowledge related to their craft and expressed their ideas through the writings of a team (Miller, 1990) or as individuals (Grumet, 1988; Witherell and Noddings, 1991).

Not only is there a rich written tradition related to issues of self-awareness through autobiography, biography, and action research, there is also an oral tradition that has been cited in the literature. In women's studies, for example, self-awareness frequently comes from the important underlying concept of consciousness-raising, which "refers to the experience of recognizing through contact with other women (reading, research, discussion) how male-centeredness has affected the individual woman" (Richardson and Taylor, 1993, p. 2). It seems essential to us that we help to raise the consciousness of not only women, but also whomever we prepare for the classrooms of our nation's schools so that these new educators have the maturity and insight necessary to understand themselves and then be ready to deal with the knowledge of others.

If we start with the majority (white females) in teacher education under the rubric of gender, then issues of power, language, voice, empowerment, hierarchy, patriarchy, and socialization can begin to be addressed. Others in the classroom who are male or of color must also have the chance to explore themselves. They will constitute the other voices within the classroom and will express diverse ideas that need to be heard.

If we also start with the predominant white, male, school administrators, there is a need for men in the field of educational administration to deal with the concept of gender and what it is to be a man in this era. For example, it is important to work through what the privileges and burdens are that white men must deal with in the 1990s.

Because the theme is diversity, once gender has been discussed, it is possible to layer on the categories of social class, ethnicity, and other areas of difference. Student teachers and administrators in training need to know their own backgrounds—they need to have a sense of where their own families came from and, through this reflection, ascertain where many of their values were derived.

Autobiography is an excellent way to deal with the categories of gender, social class, ethnic/racial issues, and other areas of difference. Through autobiography, students can reflect on critical incidences related to categories of diversity. Once they have spent time on self, then it is time for them to begin to view others as the stage is set for studying other voices.

THE BOOK'S STRUCTURE

Because the concept of diversity as it relates to education is such a complex one, in the next chapter we will highlight some definitions that have helped us make sense of this area. We will also describe a few models that various writers in this field have developed that may assist you in understanding this concept. Following this, we will turn to knowledge bases that undergird diversity. To do this, we will describe different categories of diversity and indicate how they have been biologically, environmentally, and socially constructed and how we can attempt to reframe them for this era and the future. When we use the term diversity, we define it as an inclusive term dealing with cultural diversity and learning diversity. Under the rubric of cultural diversity, we will include the categories of sex and gender, sexual differences, social class, and ethnicity and race. Under the concept of learning diversity, we will include the more individual dimensions of learning styles, multiple intelligences, and exceptionalities.

Following the sections relating to knowledge bases of diversity, we will view this concept in various ways as it relates to education. To do this, we will relate diversity to education from a number of perspectives, taking into account the importance of autobiography, pedagogy, action research, postmodernism, and social reconstructionism.

Throughout the book, we will point out ways to reframe aspects of diversity to make them more positive rather than negative. We ask you to not only be a reflective reader but an active one as well. As you read, reflect on your own personal life and the critical incidences that shaped your perspectives on categories of diversity, perhaps using the Prologue for this book as a guide. Then think of people whom you have known who may fit the categories we describe as you read through the knowledge bases dealt with in the next sections. Be prepared to read the "new scholarship" on diversity, cited throughout the book, in areas that may have an impact on your own life and/or the lives of your students. Beyond this, we also ask you to be critical of how society, and its institutions (such as the school) has defined diversity and socially constructed categories within it.

In the past, many students have thought themselves to be inferior to others because of, for example, their inability to learn in traditional ways or their inability to study because they had no quiet place in which to learn due to the problem of poverty. Through this book and the writings cited within it, it is hoped that you may now be able to offer these students explanations for some of their difficulties, taking into account categories related to learning differences or cultural differences that have made them feel inferior and/or define themselves as "others." By understanding and working through the categories of difference yourself, there will be a chance that you can offer your diverse students in the 21st century a world full of possibilities rather than a universe full of problems.

CHAPTER 1

Definitions, Models, and Aspects of Diversity

INTRODUCTION

ONE OF THE central problems that we encountered in planning this book was arriving at a scheme to organize and structure the various topics that we wanted to include. Our goal was to be as inclusive as possible in our choice of topics but to avoid a laundry list approach. Moreover, it became evident in reviewing the rapidly expanding literature in this field, that there are multiple perspectives and varying definitions of this area, which make a single integrated presentation problematic. As an overview, therefore, we thought it best to present various definitions and models and then present our own organizing scheme as an introduction to the book.

DEFINITIONS

Presented below are a series of definitions that were taken from current books and articles in this area. We have included definitions of "multicultural education" because there is a great deal of overlap between this term and the term "diversity."

(*1*) From Banks and Banks (1993),

> Multicultural education is at least three things: an idea or concept, an educational reform movement, and a process. Multicultural education incorporates the idea that all students – regardless of their gender and social class and their ethnic, racial, or cultural characteristics – should have an equal opportunity to learn in school. (p. 3)

(*2*) From Sleeter and Grant (1988),

> . . . We will use the term multicultural education to refer to educational practices directed toward race, culture, language, social class, gender, and handicap, although in selecting it we do not imply that

> race is the primary form of social inequality that needs to be addressed. (p. 26)

(*3*) From Cushner, McClelland and Safford (1992),

> . . . Recent conceptions of diversity are expanding to include differences based on gender, ethnicity, race, class, culture, age and handicapping condition. . . . We do not equate diversity with a notion of "other." Rather, we begin with the proposition that all Americans are, to some degree, multicultural because they live in a multicultural society. (p. xvii)

We could expand this list of definitions several times, but such an expansion would merely reinforce the central issues presented in the three examples above. It is evident, for example, that almost every definition of diversity (or multicultural education) focuses on groups who have been historically marginalized in American education or for whom American schools have not, and are not, functioning very well. One of the core issues that we faced in writing this book was how inclusive our list of topics would be and whether one concept should be made more central than any other. That is, current presentations of diversity are either synonymous with, or extensively overlap with, presentations of multicultural education. All such presentations include discussions of race, gender, social class, ethnicity, and culture (to the extent that culture and ethnicity are treated as distinguishable topics). Some presentations also include handicapping condition and language, while relatively few contain topics such as giftedness and learning disability. Moreover, some of the presentations are focused on a central characteristic (e.g., race) around which the remaining themes revolve.

It is our belief that the most defensible position for educators is to use the term diversity. Moreover, we believe that multicultural education, while very similar to diversity, is not synonymous with it, but is rather a subset of this more inclusive area. In a previous publication (DuCette, Shapiro, and Sewell, in press) we have defined diversity as

> . . . encompassing the domain of human characteristics which affect an individual's capacity to learn from, respond to, or interact in a school environment. These characteristics can be overt or covert, recognized by the individual or not recognized, and biologically or environmentally or socially determined. Some of the characteristics are meaningful only as they describe an individual; others are more meaningful as they describe a group. (p. 6)

As we have already mentioned, it is our intention to make this definition as inclusive as possible without so broadening the discussion that the presentation becomes unmanageable. Thus, human characteristics such as race, gender, and intelligence are all aspects of diversity that we will include in this book because each affects an individual's capacity to function in a school environment. On the other hand, hair color (to use an extreme example) is an overt human characteristic. It is not, however, a legitimate topic to include in a discussion of diversity because there is no evidence that a person's hair color affects his or her school learning. At the end of this chapter we will present the way we have organized the topics in this book.

MODELS OF DIVERSITY

What is fascinating about the area of diversity is that each of us enters it at different starting points and with different knowledge bases. To reinforce this point, we would like to return to the three biographies presented in the Prologue. In the case of Joan's story, initially she began her journey with Judaism as her main category of being different. For her, being Jewish in an Italian city made her feel unique. Her sense of belonging, as well as her feelings of difference, came through her ethnic group. It was much later in life, however, that the category of gender made its appearance as an important factor in defining herself.

In Trevor's story, growing up in Jamaica raised his consciousness to the issue of social class. There he saw people of color rise to prominence. He felt that it was primarily the lack of educational opportunities that impeded his family's progress rather than their color. In the United States, race took on a new dimension as there were no longer many role models of people of color in important positions. For Trevor, race began to loom large as he dealt with the realities for the first time of being a minority as a person of color.

In Joe's story, ethnicity too was strong and made him feel that he belonged. However, being Catholic did not make him feel different, as many others around him were of the same religion and had similar backgrounds. It was during his college years that differences made their appearances. For Joe, moving from just being a human being to becoming a person with different characteristics took time. It also took him time to awaken to categories of difference in those other than himself.

In each of our cases, we entered upon the road to understanding and appreciating diversity from very different starting points and with different knowledge bases. Additionally, what was an important category of difference at one stage of our development, sometimes became less significant as we grew older. For the visual learner, we thought it might be useful to present different models of diversity that we have considered as we reflected upon this complex area.

One model which we have considered approaches diversity through a process of addition. That is, some aspect of diversity serves as a base on which other aspects are added. In Joan's case, a baseline could be ethnicity through her identification of her Jewishness in her childhood. Layered on top of that would be race, social class, gender, and other areas of difference. Such a model might be seen as additive (Figure 1.1).

However, there is a tendency, by using an additive or layering model, to picture the growing awareness of different categories of diversity as simplistic and incremental. This is not necessarily the case. Frequently, dynamics occur as one kind of difference intersects with another. These intersections have the potential to cause profound changes rather than incremental changes in a person. In the case of Joe, although ethnicity in the form of the Catholic faith formed a baseline for his world view, the categories of gender, social class, and other areas of difference intersected with his view of self and others as he matured and interacted with those who were different from himself. Gay (1994) designed a model that might fit Joe's and many of our own views of difference. In Gay's model[1] (Figure 1.2), race/ethnicity forms a solid baseline enabling her to become aware of various areas of difference intersecting with the baseline.

However, Gay's model does not provide any hierarchy of variables other than that of race/ethnicity, which is at her core. Her model might be modified if one looks at Trevor's story. While in Jamaica in his early

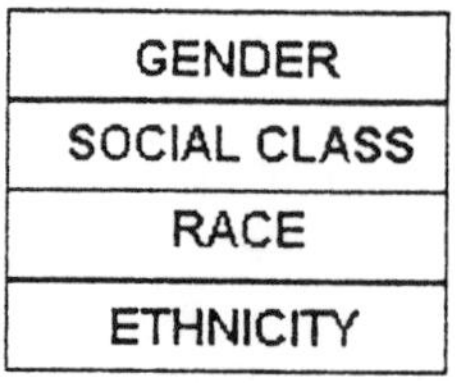

GENDER
SOCIAL CLASS
RACE
ETHNICITY

Figure 1.1.

[1]*Note:* Most of the models depicted in this chapter are derived from presentations at the Multicultural Infusion Center. Details about this center are presented in the Appendix.

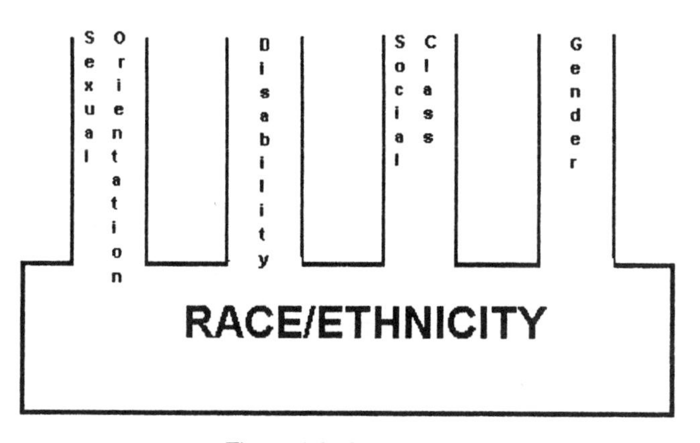

Figure 1.2 *Gay's model.*

life, social class formed a baseline; but over time, especially after he moved to the United States, race/ethnicity began to form the base for his world view. In his case, perhaps, two baselines (social class and race/ethnicity) might be useful with other variables of difference intersecting with those baselines (Figure 1.3).

Another way to modify Gay's model would be to create a hierarchy of other categories by creating not only baselines, but by making the lines that intersect represent different degrees of importance. In the case of a person who has been brought up in poverty and whose baseline is social class, race/ethnicity and disability might well be very important

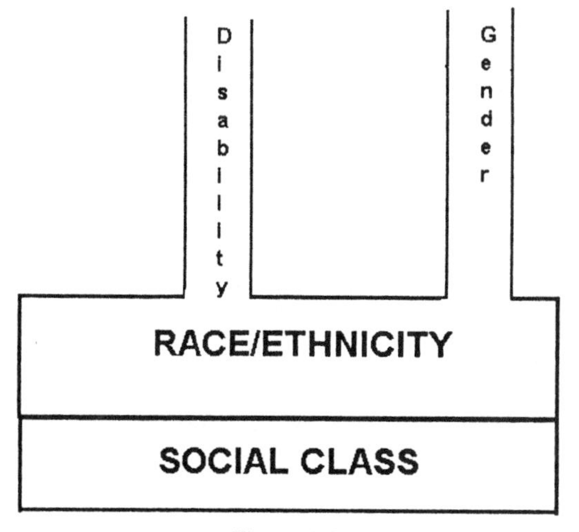

Figure 1.3.

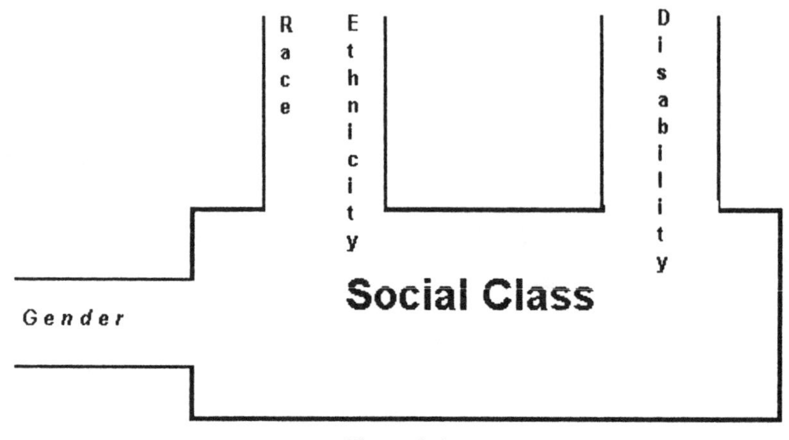

Figure 1.4.

factors over time. In that case, these two factors might be located at central points on the baseline. Other variables, such as gender, may seem less salient to this person and might intersect with social class somewhere off to the side (see Figure 1.4).

Terry Tafoya (1994) has a different model in mind when he thinks of aspects of diversity. Tafoya pictured overlapping domains that contain important categories of difference to an individual. He has gone so far as to label one domain as a series of question marks, which indicates that there is a possibility that yet another area of difference might become salient in a person's life over time (see Figure 1.5).

However, when one pictures the concept of diversity, it is important

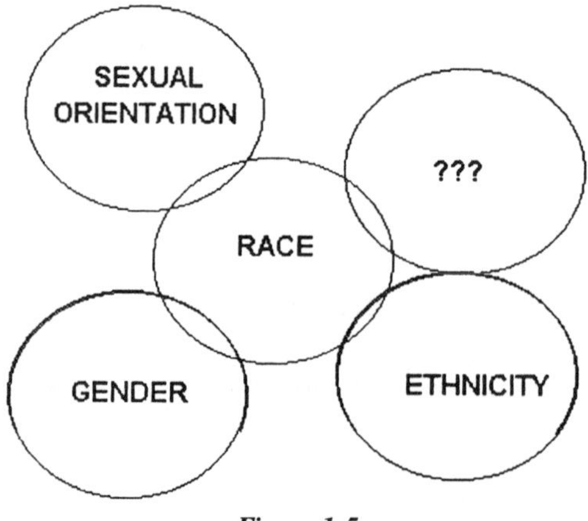

Figure 1.5.

that the complexity of this area is noted. Above all, the starting points and the knowledge bases initially selected to study this challenging area need to be taken into account. When selecting a book or materials to read in the area of diversity, it is important to take into account the author's frame of reference or baseline, and the literature that is cited. Usually a pattern emerges, and it is possible to interpret the author or authors' model(s) of diversity. This analysis can lead to more of a reflective and sophisticated understanding of this interdisciplinary and comprehensive area.

DIFFERENCES IN KIND/DIFFERENCES IN DEGREE

To reiterate a point we made earlier, we wanted to avoid simply listing a series of variables that affect student learning. As a consequence, we have attempted to devise a structure through which the various aspects of diversity could be presented. Although there are undoubtedly many alternate ways to do this, the one that seemed to be most inclusive and that made the fewest theoretical assumptions was to divide the various aspects of diversity into two groups. We have called these two broad groupings "differences in degree" and "differences in kind," recognizing that any way of characterizing the various kinds of diversity will probably produce problems for some readers. To avoid some of these definitional problems, we are making the following distinction.

There is a group of individual difference variables that is conceptualized as continua or dimensions – intelligence and learning styles are two clear examples. For these variables, all people are seen as falling along a continuum, and, in most cases, it is possible to assign a number to each individual representing the strength (or amount of presence) of that characteristic for that person. In general, many of these variables are derived from psychology, and the issue of operational definition is almost always central. That is, most of these constructs are assessed through some form of standardized, often paper-and-pencil, test.

Conversely, there are other constructs for which the concept of a continuum is largely meaningless – race, gender, and ethnicity are three examples. To a great extent, these variables are more often the focus of disciplines involving the study of groups, such as sociology and anthropology, and the issue of operational definition is often irrelevant. Although these differences in kind share the underlying theme of tapping an aspect of diversity, they are quite different in the way they are discussed in the educational literature.

One way of capturing the differences between these two types of diversity is to recognize that many of the variables that we have included under the rubric of differences in degree are viewed as having relatively direct effects on achievement. Thus, a student's intelligence, learning style, or learning disability is conceptualized differently from variables such as race or gender. For these latter characteristics, it is assumed that their effects are indirect. That is, girls may not achieve at the same rate as boys in science because the typical science textbook is written in such a way that girls' interests or learning styles are inadequately addressed (see the chapter on gender later in this book). To use a traditional distinction from research methodology, differences in degree are often treated as independent variables, whereas differences in kind are often moderator variables.

We realize that this scheme has problems, and we recognize that not all aspects of diversity fit neatly into one or the other of these groups. Nevertheless, we felt that this structure was a solution to the difficult issue of finding commonalities among variables that, in fact, are derived from different theoretical bases and that ask very different questions and pose very different solutions to educational problems.

We view the distinction we are making to be similar to the distinction made by Reynolds (1988). In his chapter, "Students with Special Needs," Reynolds distinguishes between individual differences conceptualized as categories versus those conceptualized as variables. He cites as an example of categories such groups as "retarded" or "disturbed," whereas "chronological age" and "IQ" are examples of variables. Although Reynolds intended his discussion to be relevant only to special education, and he was largely critical of the categorical labelling of children, the essential classification he has made seems to us to be useful in our presentation.

PART I

Differences in Kind

IN THIS PART of the book, we will present a series of variables that we have termed differences in kind. As we mentioned in Chapter 1, these are variables that divide people into relatively large groups: men and women, African-Americans, Asians, Latinos, Caucasians, etc. It is assumed in this type of analysis that the differences between these macrogroups are larger than the differences within them. As we will note, this assumption is not always true and not always accepted. Still, these variables represent the core of what is often called "multicultural education," and their inclusion in a book on diversity is both obvious and mandatory.

We have decided to begin this section with an extended presentation of sex and gender in Chapter 2. We have chosen this area because it seems to capture most of the central issues for variables of this type, and also because so much current attention is focused on these constructs especially as they relate to schooling. We will then present in Chapter 3 a series of other variables (race, social class, sexual differences, and ethnicity), which, in our frame of reference, are similar to sex and gender, as we regard them as differences in kind.

CHAPTER 2

Sex and Gender

INTRODUCTION TO SEX AND GENDER

WE BEGIN THIS section of the book by examining the large and growing literature on sex and gender and their relationship to educational outcomes. These related and overlapping topics would seem to be a logical starting point for this section of the book for several reasons. First, despite the gains in the women's movement over the past twenty years in the United States, the traditional patterns of women as teachers and men as managers of schools persist. Currently, nearly 69 percent of teachers in the United States are women (85 percent of elementary, 53 percent of middle/junior high school, and 44 percent of secondary) (National Center for Education Statistics, 1989), and approximately 75 percent of school administrators are men (88 percent of secondary principals and 66 percent of elementary principals) (Jones and Montenegro, 1990). It is as true today as it has been for the last 100 years that almost all children in this society spend a majority of their formative years in institutions in which women teach and men manage. Because this situation consequently creates environments that are highly structured according to sex (or gender, depending on one's theoretical orientation), it is obviously important to understand the effects this environment has on students' learning from a cognitive and an affective perspective.

Another reason for beginning this section on the topics of sex and gender is that these constructs represent, perhaps better than most, the dramatic shift in emphasis that has occurred during the last twenty to thirty years in the way certain variables are treated in the educational literature. Traditionally, the topic of differences between girls and boys was listed in textbooks under the heading of "sex differences" and the discussion always included, indeed focused upon, such biologically based outcomes as differences in rate of development and possible genetic variations in certain achievement domains (e.g., mathematics, science, and verbal skills). As we shall see in reviewing the current literature, the essential nature of the discourse in this area has changed along two lines. First, many feminist and constructivist writers attempt to demonstrate that sex differences in educational achievement are nonexistent or trivial. For these writers, whether a student is male or female should have no effect on how that student does in school. Second, where differences are shown to exist, the reason for these differences is almost always placed in an environmental rather than a biological context. In large part, then, much of the current literature focuses on gender differences and the way gender roles and expectations are constructed by our society. Nevertheless, the traditional focus on sex differences, and the confusion that often exists between sex and gender, necessitates a discussion of both constructs in a book on student diversity. More critically, we shall attempt to show at the end of this section of the book that the movement from sex to gender reflects more clearly than for any other construct the movement into postmodernism, which characterizes the work of a growing group of educational researchers.

We offer the following definition of sex and gender by Anderson (1988) as a way of structuring and focusing our discussion. According to Anderson (1988), "sex refers to the genetic and physical identity of the person and is meant to signify the fact that one is either male or female. One's biological sex usually establishes a pattern of gendered expectations" (p. 75). Anderson, when describing gender, says, "Gender refers to the socially learned behaviors and expectations that are associated with the two sexes. Thus, whereas 'maleness' and 'femaleness' are biological facts, masculinity and femininity are culturally constructed attributes" (p. 75). She goes on to say that gender is a broad concept encompassing "complex political, economic, psychological, and social relations between men and women in society" (p. 76).

A similar distinction between sex and gender is made by Archer and Lloyd (1989). According to these authors, a central component in the earlier discussions of sex differences was the desire by reductionist social science in general, and behavioral psychology in particular, to transpose the methods taken from the physical sciences into psychology. In traditional, psychometrically based psychological research, measurements taken from specific tests are used to make broader generalizations about groups. For example, if research finds a difference between men and women on a specific test that purports to measure mathematical reasoning, the conclusion is drawn that men differ from women in mathematical ability. As Archer and Lloyd (1989) comment about this approach,

> Attempts to apply such rigorous measurement of abstract psychological characteristics, in a manner analogous to measuring physical features, encounter a number of difficulties, which the social-cognitive approach highlights. This broader view of psychological testing places both the psychologist and the person taking the test in a wider social context. Each of the participants has commonsense views about the nature of men and women and about the social setting of the test. As such, the emphasis shifts from trying to define and measure general traits to examining how men and women react to the experimenter and how they perceive the test conditions and requirements. (p. 15)

Archer and Lloyd (1989) also comment about the problems of making precise distinctions between the concepts of sex and gender and indicate that the two are often difficult to distinguish. As they state,

> We believe that the distinction is often difficult to make in practice and that it implies that differences between men and women are either biologically produced or socially determined. We have already indicated the limitations of this view, which derives from commonsense notions and which seeks a reductionist explanation. Adopting a distinction based on attribution alerts us to problems. When attribution is derived from social criteria, whatever differences are subsequently found between men and women are called gender differences. In fact, biological differences would be expected to contribute to gender differences, but they would be mediated through an interaction with the environment according to a person's mental concepts—or commonsense ideas about men and women. (p. 19)

Although it is clearly too simple to say that the difference between sex differences and gender differences can be completely captured by the distinction between innate and learned (or between heredity and environment or biology and sociology), focusing the discussion this sharply can perhaps help in clarifying some of the confusing issues in this area. Both conceptually and empirically, there are always three interrelated questions that can be asked when the focus is on differences between men and women: 1) Do differences, in fact, exist? 2) If so, why? and 3) What, if any, are the educational implications of these differences?

As we said above, a noticeable change has occurred in recent years where educational effects that were once viewed as primarily sex-based are now often considered gender-related. One of the significant contributors to this movement has been the group of writers and researchers who have developed the interdisciplinary area of women's studies, which is now found on many college campuses and whose influence is rapidly spreading into high schools and elementary schools. This group has provided considerable scholarship by and about women that has paved the way for discussing how gender affects a wide range of outcomes within the school as well as within society. More broadly, the Women's Studies Movement, and the even more recent Men's Studies Movement, are both results of an essential change in the way that social science is conducted. The significant movement away from strictly positivistic and empirical methodologies has opened the way for new areas of scholarship and new ways of conceptualizing old debates. Of all the differences in kind that we will discuss in this book, therefore, the discussion and debate over gender and sex reflect most of the critical points that are being raised for the other categories included in this section.

A REVIEW OF THE RESEARCH ON SEX DIFFERENCES

The idea that women are not only different from men but are also inferior to them has historical roots in both the Christian and Jewish religions. In both religions, women were viewed as being created by God to be man's helpmate but not his equal. It is not surprising, therefore, that as science attempted to replace religion as the dominant explanatory vehicle for many biological and physical phenomena, the prevailing notion would be that differences between the sexes should be expected, and that these differences would be in favor of men. This assumption of male superiority so dominated early social science (in particular psychology) that significant differences between men and women on standardized tests, which purported to measure ability (e.g., quantitative ability, logical thinking, problem solving) rather than being conceptualized as test bias, were instead considered arguments for the tests' validity.

This assumed superiority of men over women also explains the rationale for the long series of studies (e.g., Gough and Heilbrun, 1965; Komarovsky, 1950; Williams and Bennett, 1975), which demonstrated that women were stereotyped in a far more negative way than were men. The Williams and Bennett (1975) study is typical: subjects were given a list of 300 adjectives and asked to sort them into those that described men and those that described women. Not only were the subjects able to do this with a fair amount of agreement, but a large percentage of the adjectives that were characterized as feminine were negative (e.g., complaining, weak, whiny) whereas a large percentage of the male adjectives were positive (assertive, confident, logical). It is in this context in which the long history of research and theorizing on sex differences must be viewed. If for no other reason than historical completeness, a brief presentation of this literature is in order to frame the discussion and to present the context for a discussion of gender.

One of the classic presentations in this area is Maccoby and Jacklin's *The Psychology of Sex Differences* (1974). We thought it might be instructive to present their summary of the state of this research at the time they published their volume (i.e., 1974). Maccoby and Jacklin divided the research into three groups: 1) unfounded beliefs about sex differences; 2) sex differences that are fairly well established; and 3) open questions: too little evidence, or findings ambiguous. The specific listings under each of these headings are as follows:

(*1*) Unfounded beliefs about sex differences
- Girls are more social than boys.
- Girls are more suggestible than boys.
- Girls have lower self-esteem than boys.
- Girls are better at rote learning and simple repetitive tasks, whereas boys are better at tasks that require higher-level cognitive processing and the inhibition of previously learned responses.
- Boys are more analytic.
- Girls are more affected by heredity, whereas boys are more affected by environment.
- Girls lack achievement motivation.
- Girls are auditory, boys are visual.

(*2*) Sex differences that are fairly well established
- Girls have greater verbal ability than boys.
- Boys excel in visual-spatial ability.
- Boys excel in mathematical ability.
- Males are more aggressive.

(*3*) Open questions: too little evidence, or findings ambiguous
- Do girls demonstrate higher levels of tactile sensitivity?
- Are girls more fearful, timid, and anxious?

- Are boys more active?
- Are boys more competitive?
- Are boys more concerned with dominance?
- Are girls more compliant?
- Do girls demonstrate higher levels of nurturance and maternal behavior? (pp. 347–354)

To demonstrate how this area has changed during the twenty years since Maccoby and Jacklin published their book, we need only examine the four statements listed under "fairly well established" sex differences. Of these, the first three are either no longer considered true, in that differences are no longer believed to exist, or are reinterpreted as strongly gender-related. The fourth (male aggressiveness) is still considered accurate but would probably be explained by pointing out that males have higher activity levels than females (considered a temperament variable) and that boys are socialized to resolve conflict through aggression.

The profound nature of the change in this area can be seen in a recent meta-analysis of the literature on sex differences. This review, involving thousands of studies and millions of subjects (Hyde, 1993), concluded that, at present, there are no appreciable differences between men and women in verbal ability and only a modest difference in math skills. Moreover, a recent review of gender differences in science (Kahle et al., 1993) concludes that almost all of the differences between boys and girls in science achievement result from the misperception by teachers that science is an inherently masculine discipline, involving inherently masculine skills such as analyzing and hypothesizing, and that girls are therefore permitted less access to science-related materials and curriculum. This reinterpretation of differences in achievement between male and female students is demonstrated most clearly by examining mathematical ability, an area of research that has received considerable recent attention.

Although there is disagreement about the extent of the difference, most research in the area of mathematical ability demonstrates that males score higher than females on standardized tests of mathematical ability. For example, Hyde (1993) finds about a quarter of a standard deviation difference in performance in favor of males across a variety of standardized tests, with the discrepancy somewhat larger in the upper grades. Using national data on the Scholastic Aptitude Test, Halpern [cited in Gunter and Gunter (1990)] reports a difference of about fifty points between males and females, despite recent efforts by the testing company to eliminate this discrepancy. Why does this difference exist? Several theories have been set forward to explain the discrepancy between male and female students. The clearest example of a sex-based theory is that males are superior in spatial-visualization skills, and that differences in these skills explain differences in learning (Maccoby, 1966). As might be expected in this area, both of these assertions are challenged by writers who believe that the difference in test performance (if, in fact, they accept the data indicating that there is a difference) is due to a student's gender rather than to his or her sex. Several competing theories have been forwarded: 1) differential mathematics courses taken in high school are the cause of sex-related differences in mathematics achievement (because females take fewer mathematics courses, and the level of the courses they do take is not as advanced as the level for males) (Fennema, 1984; Fennema and Sherman, 1977); 2) females perceive mathematics as less useful to them (as compared to males) in preparing for careers or in achieving social success; 3) females lack confidence in their ability to learn mathematics; 4) teachers interact differently with boys than with girls in mathematics classes; and 5) parents have lower expectations for girls than for boys regarding performance in mathematics (Jacobs, 1991).

Although these different explanations of male-female differences in performance on mathematics tests are informative in demonstrating the types of theories that have been developed in this area, the most interesting analysis is to compare the theories in regard to what they say about the possibility of eliminating these differences. The implications of choosing the position that attributes differential performance to differences in spatial-visualization skills, as contrasted to any of the other theories, is that each of the alternatives can lead to remedial solutions that would eliminate the difference in performance between men and women. That is, teaching practices could change, parents could be sensitized to their interactional patterns, or females' self-concept regarding mathematics could be improved. If, on the other hand, the difference is due to a skill deficit that is more or less genetically determined, the possibility of remediation is much less pronounced.

A specific instance of this general question has been raised by the ACLU in analyzing the results of the National Merit Scholarship competition (*Philadelphia Inquirer*, June 6, 1994). The ACLU points out that 55 percent of National Merit Scholarship participants are females, yet females constitute only 40 percent of the finalists. Because these scholarships are largely determined by the Preliminary Scholastic Assessment Test (PSAT), the ACLU argues that the difference in selection rates indicates that these tests are clearly biased against females. Moreover, females obtain higher grades in mathematics in both high school and college. Because the PSAT is designed to predict grades in college, and because females, as a group, have higher grades yet lower test scores, it follows that the validity of the PSAT is seriously damaged. As a consequence, the ACLU charges that the PSAT is unfair to girls and is working to eliminate it or to at least reduce its influence in choosing National Merit Scholarship winners.

The complexity of this issue is well captured in a recent article by Gallagher and DeLisi (1994). In their research they have found that high-ability female students use more conventional strategies to solve complex mathematical problems, whereas high-ability male students use more unconventional strategies. Although admitting that their research was not designed to answer the question of why these differences exist, they indicate that the cause may reside in a complex interaction of physiological and environmental factors:

> . . . because of both physiological differences in male and female brains and differences in socialization of male and female students, female students are generally better at tasks that require the rapid retrieval of information from memory; whereas male students are usually better at tasks that require the manipulation of information that is already represented in memory. . . . High scoring female students, as a group, seemed to be more conservative in their strategies; they relied more heavily on methods that they were taught in school. This may be caused by lowered confidence or interest or by the way they learn and think about mathematics. (p. 210)

We could elaborate on these examples many times [see, for example, Kahle's (Kahle et al., 1993) explanation of why females do not typically achieve at the same level as males in science presented at the beginning of this section]. If we view the sex/gender distinction from a political rather than a scientific perspective, we can see that questions about the existence of sex differences and the reasons for these differences are answered quite differently by writers on either side of this issue. Those who believe in sex differences assume that there are genetically based differences in capacity between males and females and that these differences cannot easily be eliminated. On the other hand, those who contend that almost all variations between the sexes are due to gender differences, believe that educationally relevant differences between the sexes are nonexistent or small, and that the variation that does exist is due to the context in which learning occurs. More importantly, they believe that group differences in achievement should be eliminated by modifying the environment so that the constraints which negatively affect female learners are removed. We will return to this political analysis at the end of this section. At this point, however, we will focus our presentation on the issue of gender differences and the implications of gender for education.

GENDER DIFFERENCES AND EDUCATION

Derived in large part from feminism and from scholarship in women's studies, a large body of research has begun to accumulate demonstrating that schools do not represent level playing fields for boys and girls. In keeping with the distinction between sex and gender that we have been making in this chapter, any such difference in the educational environment would constitute a gender-related effect. As many writers have noted, the educational environment of schools has not historically been gender-neutral, leading to biases of all kinds. In fact, Sadker and Sadker (1982) have noted as many as six forms of gender biases within the curriculum including: *linguistic bias* in which the use of generic "he" and terms such as caveman, forefathers, and mankind remain; *sex role stereotyping* in which girls and boys are described in traditional ways (i.e., boys as hunters and warriors, and girls as princesses and mothers); *invisibility in books and curriculum material* that simply omits the history and writings of women; imbalance through the use of only the male perspective in which there occurs, at best, a mere mention of trivial and mundane matters facing girls and women; *unreality in perpetuating myths* in which there is a desire to idealize institutions such as the nuclear family that hardly exist in reality; and *fragmentation of women's contributions* in which women's works are featured in a box or block in texts rather than being properly integrated into the main body of the subject matter (Banks and Banks, 1989).

In the area of instructional practice or pedagogy, a major report by the American Association of University Women (AAUW) (1991) has indicated that although it is almost two decades since Congress prohibited sex discrimination in education through the passage of Title IX, teachers continue to "have lower expectations for girls than for boys" (p. 1). In fact, in the AAUW report, a clear statement is made concerning the often unintentional but very real following problems:

> Whether one looks at preschool classrooms or university lecture halls, at female teachers or male teachers, research spanning twenty years consistently reveals that males receive more teacher attention than do females. In preschool classrooms boys receive more instructional time, more hugs, and more teacher attention. The pattern persists through elementary school and high school. (p. 68)

In many writings based on classroom research (i.e., Brown and Hoffman, 1991; Culley and Portuges, 1985; Delamont, 1983; Hall and Sandler, 1982; Klein, 1985; Maher and Schniedewind, 1987; Spender, 1982; Stanworth, 1983), what has been found is a recurrent pattern of white boys receiving more attention than white girls. The research shows that boys speak out more than girls without raising their hands; they are provided with teacher comments of praise, acceptance, remediation, and criticism much more than girls. In fact, the pattern is so prevalent that Spender (1982) has labelled the syndrome, "Make Trouble, Get Results."

The implications of differential classroom environments for boys and girls have been recently summarized by Sadker and Sadker in *Failing at Fairness* (1994). Among the negative effects they cite are the following:

(*1*) Girls enter school ahead of or equal to boys on almost every standardized test but leave high school and college behind.

(*2*) Girls score lower on the SAT and ACT tests in high school, thereby making entrance into college more difficult.

(*3*) Boys are much more likely to be awarded state and national scholarships.

(*4*) Women score lower on most tests that are used for entrance into professional schools.

(*5*) In the long run, these effects produce economic penalties that follow women after graduation. For example, careers that have a high percentage of women (such as teaching and nursing) are poorly paid.

While the area of teacher-student classroom interaction research has not focused strongly on patterns of overlapping categories such as race, ethnicity, and social class in relation to gender, a few recent studies have begun to address this issue. In the AAUW (1992) report, for example, evidence is presented that there is a difference in the kinds of interactions associated with white and black children and their teachers (p. 70). What we seem to know thus far is that stereotypes do exist. Black boys tend to be perceived less favorably by their teachers and are seen as less able than other students (Rosser, 1989). They also tend to have fewer verbal interactions with their teachers and yet are the recipients of four to ten times the amount of qualified praise ("That's good, but . . .") as other students (Harris and Carlton, 1990). With black girls, the interactions are extremely complex. "Black girls have less interaction with teachers than white girls, but they attempt to initiate interaction much more often than white girls or than boys of either race" (AAUW, 1992, p. 70). It is hypothesized that teachers may unconsciously rebuff black girls who speak out. Frequently, these children turn to peers for interactions often becoming the class enforcers or go-betweens for other students (National Science Foundation, 1990). In an even more recent study, Flanagan (1993) reviews the overlap of gender and social class and concludes, "Girls from lower SES families are at a distinct risk of being ignored as long as discussions of class exploitation do not include issues of gender segregation and vice versa, whether these discussions are about school, work, family, or their intersections" (p. 373). Despite these recent studies, however, much more research needs to be carried out dealing with not only the category of gender in the classroom but the overlapping areas of race, ethnicity, and social class. Despite the limitations, the research clearly shows that girls of all colors are not receiving the kinds of time, attention, and care that they deserve in our nation's classrooms.

Female Teachers and Administrators

Problems exist not only for girls in the classroom but also for women teachers and administrators. As we have indicated previously, despite the large number of female teachers, the majority of administrators at all levels are men. In the 1990s, the traditional patterns remain intact.

Apple (1986) and others have written extensively about the relatively powerless position of female teachers and how they have been devalued. He has written of the belief, throughout many eras, that teachers might not be professional enough to design a curriculum of their own. This lack of faith in female teachers' abilities has led to what he and others have called the teacher-proof curriculum and the de-skilling of teachers.

In the 1980s and 1990s, despite the rhetoric emphasizing the professionalization of teaching, there seem to be few attempts to raise teachers' self-awareness through education that lead to empowerment. Few opportunities for the understanding of a category as important as gender tend to exist in teacher preparation programs and in-service learning. In fact, in Sleeter's (1992) study of thirty white teachers who participated in a multicultural education staff development project, the author found many of these experienced teachers were lacking in knowledge of themselves as well as others. In addition, the teachers tended to be conservative, particularly on the issues of race and ethnicity. By the end of her investigation, Sleeter wondered if her sample of teachers understood gender discrimination issues within society at all.

Problems for women continue, not only within the classroom, but also within the administration. Although there are many female teachers, there still are few female principals and superintendents. The lack of females in leadership posts is not positive for girls. We know how important appropriate role modeling is for the young. What is so unfortunate is that there are many qualified educators in the pipeline (National Policy Board for Educational Administration, 1989; Pavan, 1985) to take on these roles. Of late, there has been some movement, simply because the number of female students in educational administration has risen drastically. It is well documented, however, that highly intelligent and experienced female educators are frequently overlooked for leadership positions (Marshall, 1985; Ortiz and Marshall, 1988; Pavan, 1985; Shakeshaft, 1987; Shapiro, 1987).

Some of the literature blames women themselves for this apparent career stagnation. Internal or psychological barriers are often cited. Blame is frequently attributed to deficiencies of credentials, degrees, and classroom experience (Shakeshaft, 1987; Shapiro, 1987). Other reasons are more psychologically oriented and include low levels of confidence and autonomy, lack of aspirations and motivation, numerous family and home responsibilities, and the effects of sex-role stereotyping and female socialization (Abbey and Melby, 1986; Marshall, 1985; Tetreault and Schmuck, 1985). Although there may be some psychological and internal obstacles that hinder their mobility, there is evidence that formidable, well-defined external factors inhibit development of female school administrators. These factors include the low level of encouragement for women to enter administrative posts, a limited number of role models, lack of networks, and discriminatory practices in hiring and promoting women (Shakeshaft, 1987; Shapiro, 1987).

Male Teachers and Administrators

Men who teach and administer in schools also have their share of issues with which they must contend as the educational environment evolves. Just as women's roles have been socially constructed by society, so have men's. Currently, men are asking themselves questions about their own position in society and are attempting to make sense of changing morals and behavior.

New literature has been making its appearance that deals with men and masculinity. Clatterbaugh (1990) presented some perspectives that he believes have begun to dominate this area of research. He speaks of six perspectives. They are: 1) *the conservative perspective* that defends the age-old position of men as providers and protectors (Gilder, 1973, 1986; Winner, 1983); 2) *the profeminist perspective* that charges men to leave behind masculinity that oppresses women and even oppresses them (Doyle, 1989; Kimmel, 1987; Pleck, 1981); 3) *the men's rights perspective* that looks at the discrimination that men face through role expectations (Diamond, 1983; Goldberg, 1987); 4) *the spiritual perspective* that focuses on men returning to their rites of passages and attempts to offer self-exploration through faith (Bly, 1981; Rowan, 1987); 5) *the socialist perspective* that turns to the works of Marx and the socialist agenda to empower men to overturn the capitalistic structure of society (Robinson, 1983; Zaretsky, 1976); and 6) *the group-specific perspective* that looks at masculinity overlapping with other categories such as race, ethnicity, and sexual orientation (Fernback, 1981; Gibbs, 1988; Munoz, 1989).

The Case for and against Single-Sex Schools and Classrooms

A specific issue within the broader discussion of sex and gender and their effects on classroom functioning, which has received considerable recent attention, is the movement for single-sex schools and classrooms. The existence of single-sex schools, of course, is hardly a recent phenomenon in America, where single-sex colleges and universities were common until the latter part of the 20th century, and where single-sex high schools, especially in the private or parochial sector, were (and still are) common. The issue has become more political in recent years because any form of exclusionary educational practice of this type runs counter to the movement for inclusive education. It is easy to understand why proponents of inclusive education (which is usually placed in the context of special education) would find segregating students into single-sex schools or classes upsetting.

Although the issues are actually quite complex, the two sides of this discussion can be set forward rather simply. Proponents of single-sex schools argue that the known effects of having males and females in the same classroom can be eliminated by having separate classes for each sex. If, for example, teachers pay more attention to males and provide a more supportive classroom climate for them, this effect could not exist if only females were being taught. The same type of argument has been proposed for the creation of classes that are not only single-sex, but also single-race. There have been, for example, several attempts to create all male, all African-American classrooms, often taught by male, African-American teachers. The rationale for this type of classroom is that the known negative stereotypes of African-American, male students (aggressive, low motivation, disruptive) would be reduced if all students were the same in a classroom environment that rejected historical stereotypes. Moreover, by placing a same-race, same-sex teacher in charge of the classroom, a positive role model would be provided.

Opponents of this position argue that any form of tracking or exclusionary practice is educationally wrong and probably illegal. They would contend that there is no empirical support that single-sex classrooms improve the achievement levels of the students in them. Moreover, these single-sex classrooms are not typical of the world outside of the classroom, so that students are not being prepared for the life they will lead when school is over.

As is so often true in debates of this type, the research supporting either side is weak and inconsistent. [See, for example, Fuller and Clarke (1994) for a presentation of some of the research on this topic.] In general, the research base is not extensive, and the findings that do exist do not provide clear support for either side. At present, this topic must remain one of the unresolved issues about whether sex or gender impact upon educational achievement. In the highly politicized arena in which this topic is now discussed, we should expect that the answer will depend on the perspective of the writer and that empirical support will not be considered the only criterion for acceptance.

IMPLICATIONS OF GENDER FOR EDUCATORS

Despite our increasing knowledge of gender issues, our awareness of sex discrimination cases, and the need for gender-fair education (Sadker and Sadker, 1982), little has changed in the preparation of the student teacher (AAUW, 1991) and the school administrator (Parker and Shapiro, 1993; Sadker, Sadker, and Klein, 1991). In fact, there continue to be few curricular reforms, pedagogical changes, staff development modifications, recruitment initiatives, career restructuring programs, and empowerment improvements targeted for girls and women in education, even if education is broadly defined. There are even fewer reforms targeted at boys' and men's roles related to the field of education.

In the area of the curriculum, the selection of textbooks and other reading matter that takes into account gender-balancing can help to combat sexism. Gender issues and imbalances should be dealt with not only in the curriculum and texts of students, but also in the texts in teacher education. It should be noted that in a 1981 analysis of teacher education texts (AAUW, 1991), a third of them did not even mention the topic of sexism.

Additionally, in the area of curriculum development, curriculum integration projects that move much of the new scholarship on girls and women into the mainstream are already being documented (Aiken et al., 1987; Arch, Kirschner, and Tetreault, 1983; Fritsche, 1984; Schmitz and William, 1983; Schuster and Van Dyne, 1985; Spanier, Bloom, and Boroviak, 1986). However, only a few of these projects are aimed specifically at the preparation of new and experienced teachers (Shapiro, Parssinen, and Brown, 1992; Styles, 1988).

Administratively, if there is an opportunity to assist in the selection of a new principal or superintendent, there should be an awareness of the need for female role models for girls (Fauth, 1984; Marshall, 1985; Shakeshaft, 1987; Shapiro, 1987). Whenever possible, women need to be encouraged to assume leadership positions as coaches, team leaders, etc. In particular, math, science, and other traditionally male areas should be taught by female teachers. On the other hand, it could be of value if male teachers taught nontraditional subjects as well as assumed more caretaking functions within schools.

Above all, gender-fair education can make a difference and can help to change attitudes and break down biases. But gender-fair education will not occur until teachers and school administrators are prepared in this area. Through a focus on female and male theories and issues in teacher training, administrative training, and in-service training programs, self-awareness can be developed. Additionally, preparation in the category of gender will enable women teachers and male school administrators, who make up the majority of educators today, to begin to understand their students' and other constituencies' needs. Such training may have a positive effect on the development of both male and female educators and it may ultimately lead to a more empathetic and understanding society.

A RETURN TO SEX AND GENDER

We want to end this section on sex and gender by returning to our comment that this topic has significant political ramifications that have impacted and continue to impact upon education. In the beginning of this book, we defined diversity as any educationally relevant variable that affects an individual's capacity to learn from, respond to, or interact in an educational environment. There can be no question that this stipulative definition encompasses sex and gender, for these aspects of self are obvious, pervasive, and enduring. We have also seen, however, that the discussion of sex and gender can move rapidly from empiricism to politics seemingly without a pause. (It can be argued, of course, that the same statement can be made about almost every meaningful concept in the educational literature. Sex and gender are perhaps only an extremely obvious case.) A clear and recent example of this movement between two perspectives occurred in a written discussion between Feingold (1992) and Noddings (1992) on the existence of sex differences in intellectual ability. We will finish this section of the book with their discussion because it captures one of the central issues in this debate.

Feingold's (1992) review summarized a large quantity of research that investigated the differences in ability between males and females. He focused almost all of his article on research using standardized tests such as the Wechsler Intelligence Scales, the California Achievement Tests, and the Differential Aptitude Tests. Feingold's main point was that, while there were at times "mean" differences between the sexes, there were almost always "variance" differences between them (at least for quantitative and spatial abilities) with males demonstrating more variability than females. That is, in general, the standard deviations of the male samples used in the norming populations for many standardized ability tests were slightly higher than the standard deviations of the female samples. His point was almost exclusively statistical, and the implications he drew from this point were centered strongly in the empiricist tradition. He states in his conclusion,

> Proponents of the greater male variability hypothesis have usually championed biological explanations for the sex differences in variability, whereas the critics of the theory have generally been environmentalists. Therefore, the causes of the findings of sex differences in variability were usually assumed to be innate, whereas sex differences in central tendency have long been recognized as being explainable by environmental as well as biological theories. This unfortunate confusion of findings with ex-

> planations for findings has transformed a seemingly objective question about sex differences in variability (which properly is an empirical rather than a theoretical issue) into an unwarranted source of controversy and a forum for debating nature versus nurture. (p. 80)

But what constitutes an unwarranted source of controversy for some is a central reason for controversy for others. Noddings (1992), in responding to Feingold, points out that the variability theory is labelled as "pernicious" by feminists because it continues a long-standing tendency on the part of male authors to view women as an undifferentiated mass, "alike and thus interchangeable, designed only for reproduction" (p. 86). She cites Nordau (1885) (cited in Dijkstra, 1986) as a particularly virulent example:

> Woman is as a rule, typical; man, individual. The former has average, the latter exceptional features . . . there is incomparably less variation between women than between men. If you know one, you know them all, with but few exceptions. (Dijkstra, 1986, p. 129)

Noddings goes further in pointing out that the variability hypothesis was used to explain why there were so few women in science and in other high-status fields, and contends that the theory was instrumental in steering women into occupations suited to their mediocre (and assumably uniform) abilities.

It is beyond the scope of this book to fully explore the issues raised by Feingold and Noddings, and the reader is referred to the original sources for a full treatment. We have included these comments here because they capture so well the sometimes parallel and nonintersecting nature of the discourse on this topic. It is interesting that in her review, Noddings questions whether this topic should be researched at all because it is so problematic and troubling to feminists. She concludes that further research is probably warranted, if for no other reason than to demonstrate that the difference in variability between men and women will decrease with time. She is, however, critical of Feingold for being "oddly neutral" about a topic, which for her and for many feminists, is so emotionally laden. In his response, Feingold says that he prefers "appropriately scientific" to "oddly neutral," and that he wants to take the entire discussion out of the realm of politics.

Whatever else might be said about the issue of sex and gender differences in the present intellectual climate, it is unlikely that the issue can ever be taken out of the realm of politics. A student's gender is an obvious marker that establishes expectations about that student on the part of teachers, administrators, and parents. It would be foolish to ignore these expectations and it is pedagogically wrong to deny them. Moreover, it is possible that there are sex differences that might affect how males and females learn at different stages of their educational careers. We know, for example, that boys typically develop physically at a slower rate than girls. All elementary teachers are aware of this biological fact, and adequate teaching at this level takes this difference between the sexes into account. On the other side of this question, there is fairly good evidence that females have poorer perceptions of their mathematical abilities. All teachers should be aware of this fact; good teachers should have strategies developed to eliminate this difference.

The central issue, therefore, should not be whether sex-based or gender-related differences exist; the real questions are why these differences exist and what can be done about them. It is one thing to note these differences, whether they be sex-based or gender-related; it is quite another to allow them to continue if they are the result of inappropriate environmental constraints that place either gender at a disadvantage. Our message throughout this book is that student diversity is an inescapable fact of classroom life and that this diversity should always be a source of strength in a classroom, not a cause for concern. Even with its long and troubling history, and even in the face of its enormous political baggage, the study of sex and gender is a legitimate and important topic for teachers, administrators, and all who are concerned about educational achievement.

CHAPTER 3

Other Aspects of Diversity Viewed as Differences in Kind

CULTURAL DIVERSITY

IN KEEPING WITH the distinction made earlier, we have called the topics included in this chapter of the book "other aspects of differences in kind." Like sex and gender, these variables divide people into seemingly homogeneous groups that are assumably similar in several critical ways. Many readers may be more comfortable with the term cultural diversity, which is used in the literature in approximately the same way that we are using differences in kind. As before, the literature is often inconsistent in the way terms are used and the meaning that is given to concepts. Culture, itself, is a term laden with meaning. For our purposes, we have chosen to define culture according to Bullivant (1989), who favors discussing it as "a social group's design for surviving in and adapting to its environment" (p. 27). If this definition is applied in an educational setting, then according to Bullivant it is necessary to teach about the "many social groups and their different designs for living in our pluralist society" (p. 27).

Bullivant stresses the importance of studying culture not only by turning to its customs, heritage, history, and aesthetic aspect but also by especially dealing with how it has survived. In so doing, issues of power, marginality, and alienation can be directly addressed. The hope is that a feeling of empowerment and the possibility of using ones own agency, no matter what culture or cultures one is a part of, can be fostered.

Consistent with the definition presented earlier, we have decided to discuss a wide variety of categories in this chapter: social class, sexual differences, ethnicity, and race. In an attempt to be more inclusive, we have also tried to move beyond the single-group studies approach. Sleeter and Grant (1988) coined this approach as "characterized by attention to a single group, for example, women, Asians, blacks, Hispanics, Native Americans, or the working class" (p. 105). The word "attention" in Sleeter and Grant's definition is pivotal as it indicates that emphasis is placed on the major category for the group. For example, as we mentioned in the previous chapter, in the area of women's studies, although other factors such as race and social class are deemed important, the foundation of this interdisciplinary area is solidly grounded in feminist scholarship, feminist theory, and feminist methodology.

However, it is important to realize that within the single-group areas of women's studies, African-American studies, and ethnic studies, the goal of many writers and academicians is not only to raise the consciousness of others to the literature and history of a single group by teaching its scholarship within a separate department or program, but also it is ultimately to transform the traditional curriculum. Transformation means that the mainstream curriculum is decentered to enable the scholarship and methodology of the single groups to be integrated into a new, inclusive curriculum.

The concept of transformation can be seen in phase or stage theory that indicates the steps needed to sensitize students and faculty to the importance of moving the study of a particular group (for example, women) from the margins into the mainstream curriculum (McIntosh, 1984; Schuster and Van Dyne, 1985; Tetrault, 1989). It can also be found in the Afrocentric vision of Asante (1987) and in the levels of ethnic content integration described by Banks and Banks (1989). In all of these areas, there is an effort to bring the "new scholarship," the writings and methodologies of previously neglected groups emanating from the single-study areas, into the mainstream curriculum of the schools.

In attempting to pull together salient single-group and other pertinent studies that encompass two or three aspects of cultural diversity, it becomes immediately evident that a number of these differences tend to overlap. The intersection of race and social class issues, for example, can make for different kinds of diversity from those in which gender and social-class issues combine. The complexities of overlapping differences continue to create problems in the literature on cultural diversity.

One of the reasons for this complexity has to do with what McCarthy and Apple (1988) have called the "nonsynchronous position" of groups in regard to categories such as gender, race, and ethnicity. Nonsynchrony refers to the situation that occurs when various forms of discrimination act in an asymmetrical fashion on different members of the same group. This position, developed by Hicks (1981), held that "individuals or groups in their relation to their economic and political systems do not share similar consciousness or similar needs at the same point in time'' (p. 25). This phenomenon has often meant that areas of difference, such as social class, race, and/or gender, sometimes conflict in educational settings (Parker and Shapiro, 1993).

It is important for those who prepare future educators to realize the complexities in this area of cultural diversity. We believe it is especially salient because the 1990s represents a time when there is ''a striking discontinuity between teacher and student diversity'' (Grant and Secada, 1991). There is also a striking discontinuity between school administrator and student diversity. In both of these cases, demographic information clearly shows that although the student population is becoming increasingly more diverse than ever before, the teaching force is remaining predominately white, female, and upwardly mobile working class (Apple, 1986; DeLyon and Widdowson Migniuolo, 1989; Grant and Secada, 1991; Sleeter, 1992). Additionally, despite the student population's diverse composition, school administrators continue to be predominately white, male, and middle class, although there are a growing number of white, female, middle-class educators preparing for school administrative posts (Jones and Montenegro, 1990). While it is clearly important to recruit teachers and administrators from diverse backgrounds, it is equally important to be cognizant of the homogeneity of the current and future population of professional educators and to be aware that there are striking discontinuities between these educators and the students they teach.

It follows from these striking discontinuities that a major task of educational programming is to provide the predominately white, female, upwardly mobile, working-class teachers and the white, male, middle-class school administrators with knowledge of diverse groups to develop in them an understanding of differences. In most cases, we also hope that with understanding will come a sense of appreciation of and empathy for those differences. Along with this understanding, appreciation, and empathy towards differences, we also believe that it is exceedingly important to provide student teachers and administrative interns with a strong sense of self. We concur with Sleeter and Grant (1988) who have said that ''people must first understand themselves before they can hope to understand others'' (p. 126). If we do not succeed in this endeavor we will not have prepared our current educational students properly for the majority of American classrooms and schools in the 21st century (AAUW, 1992; Grant and Secada, 1990; Sleeter and Grant, 1988).

SOCIAL CLASS

Introduction to Social Class

Because social class has been defined in a variety of ways, we have decided that the goals of this chapter are best served by using a broad-based and somewhat less-focused definition rather than one that is clearly operationalized but narrow. We agree with Parker and Shapiro (1993), Trent (1988), and others who have noted a distinction between socioeconomic status and social class in discussions of educational issues. The former term has been associated with stratification and has been typically measured by characteristics such as family background, prestige of occupation, and economic status. The latter term has been defined as a large category of people who are of a similar socioeconomic status, but who also share commonalities in terms of lifestyles, attitudes, and cultural identification. For our purposes, then, the term social class is preferable to socioeconomic status because it better captures the issues related to educational practice.

In the United States, it is noteworthy that social class is frequently ignored as an important category in the discussion of cultural diversity. Perhaps this is the case because of the myth that the term middle class is all-inclusive and relates to most citizens. Rose (1974) believes that the majority of Americans do not want to be part of the lower social class and few think they are wealthy enough to be considered upper class. Hence, most claim that they are somewhere in the middle. Nevertheless, according to Reich (1992) there is a growing segregation of Americans by income, lifestyles, and values. In fact, he has written,

> There is only one thing Americans increasingly have in common with their neighbors, and their commonality lies at the heart of the new American "community." It is their income levels. You can bet without much risk that you earn about the same amount as the folks down the street. Your educational backgrounds are similar, you pay roughly the same amount in taxes, and you indulge the same consumer impulses. The best definition of "community" is now the zip code used by direct-mail marketers to target likely customers. (p. 277)

Despite the perception of "middle-classness" held by many Americans, the reality is that this social-class group is decreasing and that there are more poor people and more rich people than ever before in this country (Reich, 1992). Things are so polarized that at least one-fourth of all preschool children in the United States now live in poverty (Hodgkinson, 1992).

Whether we wish to admit it or not, social-class issues loom large in regard to schooling. Biemiller (1993), in reviewing the data on socio-economic status effects on academic achievement, argues that many of the differences noted in the research are, in fact, attributable to school practices such as grouping. Moreover, inequalities in school support have reached epidemic portions. Great disparities exist in the amount of money spent per student and the amount paid to teachers if a comparison between urban and suburban school districts is made. In an era in which social-class issues need to become explicit, educators must obtain an appreciation of the complexity of these issues to better understand their own institution and its place in the community.

The Tension between Equity and Excellence

There are a number of issues that immediately arise when social class is investigated in the context of schooling. One of these is the tension between equity and excellence. A central element of American consciousness is the belief in equity that is captured by the metaphor of the "melting pot." This metaphor holds that American society is structured in such a way that most immigrants are able to come to the United States, be educated as Americans in American schools, and ultimately succeed. This concept is played out in the focus on public schools as centers to bring together students from diverse social classes under one roof. Although we have given lip service to this metaphor, the current reality of the public schools is far different. In fact, where one lives has very much governed what the neighborhood school's composition will be. Despite the inequities, there are the hopes that schools will be the salvation of our society (Sarason, 1985) and that education can be the best weapon for fighting poverty and crime (Hodgkinson, 1992).

Along with a belief in equity through schooling, there is also a belief in excellence in education. Excellence in schooling is often mentioned in eras of "perceived scarcity" when there are dwindling resources and when it becomes important to determine who in fact should receive the most rigorous and most extensive education (Oakes, 1990). Meritocracy is frequently used to rationalize this concept so that the system and the rules appear to be fair. Americans want to believe that the contest is a fair one and that all have an opportunity to achieve despite their social class. In reality, however, excellence (as it is usually defined and operationalized in these debates) often proves to be the opponent of equity (Oakes, 1990), and students from working-class backgrounds tend frequently to be major victims of the battle. This tension between equity and excellence cannot help but form a backdrop to any discussion of social class and schooling in the United States.

An abiding faith in excellence in education, to the detriment of equity, can be seen in the perspective of the functionalists. These writers view schools as the major mechanism enabling the best and the brightest to be chosen for future occupational and leadership positions in society. Writers such as Blau and Duncan (1967) contended that schools are the major means by which students are socialized into their future roles in society and have provided rationales for the creation of American leaders through schooling.

A position similar to the functionalists has been put forward by the structuralists. Bowles and Gintis (1976), for example, demonstrated how social-class membership affects a person's place in society and theorized that schools reproduce society's social classes within their classrooms. Writers such as Apple (1982), Ferguson (1984), Shapiro (1990), and many others have offered a model of the economic reproduction of society within schools. To these writers, the schools mirror the greater society, preparing students to fill differentiated roles as workers in society. Gordon (1982) argued that "the normal function of schooling is to produce labor-power according to the demands of capital by making differentiated school knowledge available to advantaged and disadvantaged groups. This in turn reproduces hierarchy, exclusion, and inequality between social class and ethnic groups" (p. 90).

By advantaged, Gordon was referring to those who already come from privileged economic backgrounds. These children come to school with a significant head start, which is then reinforced through school knowledge that prepares them for the tests that will offer them access to financially rewarding careers in the future. By disadvantaged, he was speaking of the children from poverty who have not had the economic supports at home and who then come to school only to find their options limited by the courses that they are prepared to enroll in, the tests they are ready to take, and the role models they meet.

Other scholars have turned to more of a cultural reproductive argument rather than an economic reproductive argument to explain the replication of social classes within schools. Bernstein (1982), Bourdieu (1977), Wexler (1982), and others argued that the cultural and linguistic learning disseminated by the school reflected the same values and beliefs found in the dominant society.

Social-class issues in the schools have also been raised by writers who have discussed resistance theory. Anyon (1987), MacLeod (1987), Willis (1977), and others have written about the situation when people from one class, usually the lower class, tried to subvert the dominant values in the school and society. Those who resisted tended often to be the brighter students who felt that the dominant system did not understand them or reward them (Fine, 1989, 1991). A number of the students felt that completing school would not enable them to move upwards to the middle class. In fact, they believed that school was merely encouraging them to continue on in their lower-class existence; in effect, they were being prepared to know their place in society. To avoid the schooling-class-reproduction repetition in many schools, patterns of resistance tended to emerge.

One pattern that has usually led to the reproduction of social classes within the school has been tracking. Unfortunately, although tracking is frequently discussed in teacher education, it is seldom considered from a social class or critical perspective. By critical perspective, we mean the ability to view education through something other than the dominant culture's lens. The work of cultural and economic reproduction occurs through the concept of tracking when certain students are only allowed certain knowledge because they are in a lower track. Oakes (1990) has critically looked at this concept of tracking and has seen it as a way to keep children in their place. She contended that the procedure used to identify, label, regroup, and instruct children tended to lead to a control of knowledge that made it hard for them to ever catch up with children placed in a higher track.

The study of tracking leads to a discussion of what has been termed the hidden curriculum. The hidden curriculum has frequently operated through friendship networks or through social-class cliques. This curriculum, which is not taught formally, prepares students by providing information for testing, for career opportunities, and for further education. Anyon (1987), Apple (1982), Giroux (1983), McLaren (1989), Purpel (1989), and many others discovered the hidden curriculum that has quietly operated in schools and has frequently tended to be advantageous for white, middle-class students and disadvantageous for lower-class children of all colors.

Wexler's (1982) approach was slightly different from those who studied the hidden curriculum. He moved beyond the reproduction of society's social and economic order within schools, looking away from passive acceptance of these realities, towards more of an interventionist approach. This interventionist approach meant that educators needed to understand what they do to replicate the system of social class within their institutions, and then they needed to do something to change the status quo. Welch (1985) also moved in the direction of involvement in changing schools. In her case, she asked community leaders to hear the voices of working-class students and respond more to their needs through the creation of what she has called, "communities of resistance and solidarity." Another way that social class has been studied is through ethnographies and case studies of schooling (Lubeck, 1985; MacLeod, 1987; McNeil, 1986; Perry, 1988; Weis, 1990). These studies take into account the context of schools and demonstrate how social class emerges as a salient category. Many of the concepts previously discussed such as economic reproduction, cultural reproduction, resistance theory, tracking, and the hidden curriculum are also found in these case studies. They create a powerful illustration of forms of social control that keep the social classes in their place within the school.

Implications of Social Class for Education

If educators are exposed to the concept that knowledge is reproduced through social and economic means, they have already begun a critique of schooling. Additionally, if they have dealt critically with the concept of the control of knowledge through tracking, then social-class issues have been infused somewhat into the curriculum. Further, in those programs that deal with the hidden curriculum, the stage is set for a review of the writings of others who think and write of oppressed people as they relate to education. For example, the work of such educators as Anyon (1987), Friere (1970), Giroux (1983), McLaren (1989), Purpel (1989), Shapiro (1990), and many others may be incorporated into the curriculum to show how social class affects education.

Beyond a critique of schooling and the way social class affects educational outcomes, educators need to also be aware of changing demographics and the development of the underclass in American society. Through the 1990 U.S. Census, we know that the number of poor children is increasing and that at least one-half of the disabled people in our society are not able to obtain employment. Further, if we turn to Philadelphia as an example of one city's problems with an increasing underclass, data tell us that at least 2,500 children with their parent(s) live in homeless shelters each year (Philadelphia Citizen for Children and Youth, 1989). Data also indicate that 13,000 children who entered public schools in 1990 came from a home with no father present (Yancey, Goldstein, and Webb, 1987). Additionally, data reveal that 18,000 or 17 percent of preschool children are at-risk because of high levels of lead in their home and in the local environment (Philadelphia Citizens for Children and Youth, 1989).

Philadelphia's statistics are not that different from other large cities' and according to Sewell (1990), the situation is worsening. Sewell, DuCette, and Shapiro (1991) expressed their concerns about the environment for underclass and even lower-class children in the following way:

> The social reality into which many children from culturally diverse backgrounds are born must be understood as a significant factor–It is a world in which their lives are battered by poverty, social isolation and often racial and ethnic inequities. It is an environment where crime, drug addiction, pollution and abuse are daily realities. There are urban and rural communities where children attend school physically and psychologically unprepared to learn. There are social conditions in which the nutritional status and health care needs of the children adversely affect academic achievement. It is a grim world far removed from the environment of America's privileged middle and upper class youth. It is a world in which taking and doing well on a standardized test is often irrelevant and sometimes impossible. It is a world in which children attend school from environmental conditions which make learning an insignificant objective compared with the issues of personal survival. (pp. 6–7)

In his book, *Savage Inequalities,* Kozol (1991) has also warned us of the damages wrought in not acknowledging and doing something about the inequitable environments from which an increasing number of our students come. An educator needs to be aware of the communities of poverty and fear. An educator needs to read widely in the area of social class, particularly focusing on the problems of the lower and underclasses. Clearly, there is a need for the voices of the powerless and oppressed to be recognized and heard.

One way to give educators a feeling of what others are experiencing is to turn to the case studies of schooling that are emerging and that take into account the context of diverse communities. There are a number of insightful case studies that effectively deal with social class. Case studies can simulate for future teachers what they might face within schools when they must deal with students whose backgrounds are different from their own. Analysis of cases may also help to break down myths associated with social class. Additionally, they may offer some options for ameliorating within the schools some of the grave injustices that have been inflicted by society.

For example, in a case study by Lareau (1987), the researcher carried out an investigation of family-school relationships in white working-class and middle-class communities. She discovered in her study that the teachers and principals had a certain expectation for the appropriate role of parents in the schooling process. Through interviews with parents, Lareau found that working-class parents wanted their children to do well but tended to leave the education of the child up to the teacher. Middle-class parents, on the other hand, saw themselves as partners with teachers in their child's education. In the first case, the working-class parents tended to be ill at ease in the school. Many of them had not received a high school diploma. In the second case, the middle-class parents were generally at ease with the teachers. Most were professionals in their own right and had known successes throughout their education. The different backgrounds between working-class and middle-class parents made for different behavior in parents' compliance to school requests. Lareau interpreted her study using the cultural capital model (Bourdieu, 1984). She suggested that the school take into account the difference in cultural backgrounds before assuming that the working-class parents do not want their children to succeed. More studies, in the ethnographic tradition, are needed to begin to understand some of the misconceptions parents have of schools and schools have of parents, particularly when the category of social class is considered.

Social class should be treated as an important area for inclusion as part of the basic content for all new teachers. It is a category little understood and often compounded with other factors (i.e., race, gender, ethnicity). In this section, to avoid the nonsynchronous situation of compounding categories, we have tried to focus primarily on social class. Social class alone, as a category, is difficult to deal with and is far from simple.

It is hoped that readings in this area will offer educators ways to understand the problems affecting their students that are derived primarily from social-class issues. Understanding alone, however, will not suffice. Armed with knowledge and empathy, educators can help others surmount social-class barriers to attain further education. Education can lead to empowerment and an awareness of options that can enable lower-class students to move beyond a "language of critique" to a life full of "possibilities" (Giroux, 1992b).

SEXUAL DIFFERENCES

Introduction to Sexual Differences

By sexual differences, we are referring to broad categories of sexuality that encompass homosexuality, bisexuality, and heterosexuality. In particular, we will focus on those groups who do not fit the standard societal norm that tends to advocate heterosexuality, primarily for the traditional goal of procreation. For these groups, composed of gays, lesbians, and bisexuals, it has been a difficult struggle to be appreciated as acceptable and normal human beings in American society. In fact, it was not until the early 1970s that the American Psychiatric Association reversed its classification of homosexuals as people with mental disorders (American Psychiatric Association, 1980, p. 281). It was also not until the same era that universities and corporations adopted sexual orientation nondiscrimination clauses and many states decriminalized consensual, private, same-sex activity. Additionally, this was the time that less stereotypical depictions of gays and lesbians began to appear in the media (Nordin, 1989; Russo, 1981).

Although the definition of homosexuals was modified by the American Psychiatric Association, it did not mean that society accepted sexual differences. In the 1980s, for example, there were major legal setbacks barring lesbians and gays from military service (*Ben Shalom* vs. *Marsh,* 1988); forbidding educators from disclosing their sexual identity (*Rowland* vs. *Mad River Local School District,* 1985); retaining the sodomy statutes in numerous states; and retaining housing, schooling, and work discrimination on the basis of sexual orientation (Sears, 1993).

Despite the continuing legal barriers, numerous grass-roots organizations sprang up. In higher education, lesbian and gay organizations were recognized; lesbian and gay studies programs were developed; and lesbian and gay caucuses appeared in a number of national organizations (i.e., American Sociological Association, American Language Association, American Anthropological Association, American Educational Research Association, and the American Psychological Association). Even religious groups formed their own support groups, such as Roman

Catholic's Dignity and Episcopal's Integrity (Adam, 1987; Melton, 1989; Nordin, 1989). Additionally, the awareness of the high incidence of AIDS cases among members of the gay community led to the formation of political and emotional support groups of all kinds, including Gay Men's Health Crisis, ACT UP!, and the Quilt. These groups created a sense of identity and concern for those of different sexual orientations.

Sexual Differences and Schooling

The schools were slower than higher education to recognize the area of sexual differences. However, by the late 1980s, with the awareness of AIDS, the growth of other communicable diseases, and the help of Surgeon General Dr. Everett Koop, sex education courses were introduced in greater number in the nation's schools (Haffner, 1990; Sears, 1991).

Within sex education, there has been some emphasis on the study of homosexuality (Sears, 1993). There has also been a first step in the recognition of sexual diversity by a public school system in the development of The Harvey Milk School in New York City (Rofes, 1989), a school for homosexuals and their special needs. Further, gay-affirmative counseling in public high schools has been introduced with Project 10 in Los Angeles (Sears, 1989).

The need to study and understand sexual differences has been made more urgent by the release of demographic data that indicate that sexual-minority youth are at high risk. The U.S. Department of Health and Human Services has indicated that one in three lesbian and gay youths attempt suicide; one in four have serious substance abuse problems. Additionally, not only do lesbian and gay youths hurt themselves, they are also subject to stigmatization and verbal and physical assaults by peers. Violence also haunts them not only in the school yard but also in their homes, where they are frequently abused for their sexual orientation by family members (Tabor, 1992, p. 44).

In fact, the situation has reached such proportions that the Association for Supervision and Curriculum Development (ASCD), a large organization of educators, passed a resolution in 1990 that encouraged its members to "develop policies, curriculum materials, and teaching strategies that do not discriminate on the basis of sexual orientation." They also urged the schools to provide staff development training and materials to help teachers work more effectively with this "at-risk student population'' (Association for Supervision and Curriculum Development, 1990).

The resolution by the ASCD was the first time that a national educational organization had made the category of sexual minority visible. It recognized that this particular group has special problems that should be the concern of educators. Like other high-risk groups, these youngsters tend to have ''drug/alcohol problems, discipline problems, eating disorders, and youthful suicides; these students often report a history reflecting more fundamental problems such as school curriculum irrelevant to their sexual and personal needs, family problems, and lack of self-esteem and personal security'' (Sears, 1993, p. 112).

Implications of Sexual Differences for Education

Despite the growing awareness of the need for the study of sexual differences in schools, the progress in this area has been slow. Textbooks, other than in the field of sex education, tend to ignore the area of sexual orientation. Even in sex education many of the books are usually superficial. Discussions of this topic continue to be within the hidden curriculum of schools and often are dealt with in unpleasant discussions in the hallways and locker rooms (Sears, 1993). Unless addressed in a formal classroom setting, the prejudices, misinformation, distrust, and guilt will continue. Unless addressed in a sensitive and informed way, the attacks on gay youths will continue.

For the preparation of student teachers and for in-service teacher training, gay and lesbian studies can provide useful and important reading materials. Books such as *Lesbian/Women* and *The Gay Mystique* can be invaluable resources not only for sex education classes but for literature, history, and other courses in schools. Additionally, case studies make for excellent teaching devices. Eric Rofes' *I Thought People Like That Killed Themselves,* the true story of a homosexual, high school sophomore in Pennsylvania who committed suicide, could serve as an excellent starting point for a discussion of sexual diversity in the classroom. Comparing and contrasting such a book with Sylvia Plath's *The Bell Jar,* for example, could make for fascinating and important discussions within a language arts classroom.

Educators need to be aware that there are many ways to introduce this material into the classroom. Just the introduction of these topics from time to time could make an important difference to a youth who feels isolated, angry, depressed, and silenced. Works by Rich (1979, 1983) "Compulsory Heterosexuality and Lesbian Existence" and *On Lies, Secrets and Silences* can help to break the isolation and open the dialogue on sexual diversity within the classroom. History classes can also serve as places to open the discussion on sexual differences. Smith-Rosenberg's (1983) "The Female World of Love and Ritual: Relations between Women in Nineteenth-Century America," a classic article, can be used to generate an interesting debate on sexual politics and the social construction of gender over time. The readings in the area of sexual differences can break down the taboos and enable those who are different from the norm in their sexual orientation to feel engaged and involved.

While not discussing sexual differences personally, teacher educators can explore with their students heterosexuality, homosexuality, and bisexuality as topics. In so doing, teachers can help to break down the myths and prejudices surrounding sexual differences. By breaking down those myths and prejudices, high-risk students will no doubt be helped. Additionally, those who are heterosexual will feel less threatened by those who are different from themselves in the area of sexual orientation.

ETHNICITY AND RACE

Introduction to Ethnicity and Race

For the purpose of our chapter, we intend to use the umbrella term of ethnicity to encompass race. We have chosen to define ethnicity using an "expanded definition" that is recommended by Banks (1991) focusing on ethnic groups. Banks borrowed this expanded approach from Rose (1974) who wrote, "Groups whose members share a unique social and cultural heritage passed on from one generation to the next are known as ethnic groups" (p. 13). Rose expanded this definition further by saying, "Above all else, members of such groups feel a consciousness of kind and 'interdependence of fate' with those who share the customs of the ethnic tradition" (p. 13).

In his discussion, Banks (1991) included white groups such as Italian Americans or Jewish Americans, as well as ethnic groups of color. However, for the groups of color, Banks categorized them under the heading of ethnic minority groups. Often these groups tend to have "unique physical and cultural characteristics" (p. 14) that enable them to be easily classified by appearance. Although these groups are currently called minorities, the present demographic trends indicate that they will soon constitute the majority in many American cities. Hence, Banks prefers to call individuals within these groups, "people of color," and not refer to them as minorities. In this chapter, we have followed Banks' and many other scholars' preference, and we will speak of them frequently in this way.

Ethnicity seemed to us to form the perfect umbrella for this section because race is such a hard concept to categorize. As Banks wrote (1991),

> Physical anthropologists attempt to divide the human species into subgroups on the basis of biological traits and characteristics. They use the concept of race to differentiate between the various human subgroups. However, anthropologists have had considerable difficulty in trying to structure valid racial categories because of the wide variety of traits and characteristics that human groups share, the extensive mixture among groups, and because the racial categories they have formulated have been largely arbitrary. Consequently, the schemes they have developed for classifying human races vary greatly in number and in characteristics. (p. 73)

In fact, the classification of the human race is so difficult, and in many ways arbitrary, that Montagu (1974) has called it "man's most dangerous myth" (p. 9). However, when forced to, Montagu did classify humankind into four major groups: Negroid or black, the archaic white or Australoid, the Caucasoid or white, and the Mongoloid (p. 9). There are many other kinds of classifications. The U.S. Office of Personnel Management, for example, muddies the waters further by combining race with national origin and by using such categories as American Indian or Alaskan Native; Asian or Pacific Islander; black, not of Hispanic origin; Hispanic; white, not of Hispanic origin.

In many ways, it is not so much the definition of race that is important as it is the social construction of this construct that has had a profound effect and helps to create distances among human groups. Racism, derived from the way one group views another, has had powerful effects on society as a whole. According to Banks (1991),

> Racism is a belief that human groups can be validly grouped on the basis of their biological traits and that these identifiable groups inherit certain mental, personality, and cultural characteristics that determine their behavior. (pp. 74–75)

Racism as a concept has enabled such institutions as slavery to flourish and has allowed for attacks on religious groups, such as the holocaust, to be justified. Racism allowed, according to Gay (1973), attitudes to be modified into actions. As van den Berghe (1978) saw it,

> Racism was congruent with prevailing forms of capitalist exploitation, notably with slavery in the New World and incipient colonial expansion in Africa. There is no question that the desire to rationalize exploitation of non-European peoples fostered the elaboration of a complex ideology of paternalism and racism. (p. 75)

Teachers and Ethnic Groups of Color

Despite the years of focus on effective teaching, there is still a great deal that we do not know in regard to teaching students of color. According to Murrell (1991),

> There are no well-established criteria for what effective teaching looks like for minority children, nor is there clearly specified practical knowledge about teaching in urban contexts with poor minority students. Indeed, the professional knowledge associated with designing effective pedagogy with diverse populations is more apt to be viewed with awe. The popular educational literature imbues a Marva Collins or a Jaime Escalante with a special sort of pedagogical magic. They possess knowledge not immediately available to other classroom teachers until they are first demystified, decoded, and spelled out by educational researchers. As a result, we are frequently led up the short road of "teacher effectiveness" by developing decontextualized laundry lists of what expert teachers do, rather than taking the long road of clearly understanding how expert teachers acquire the contextual knowledge they possess. (p. 205)

Despite the lack of work on teacher effectiveness with regard to the needs of students of color, there is a body of work that advocates the importance of recruiting teachers of color for the future. Garibaldi (1986), Ladson-Billings (1991), Parker and Hood (1991), and others have raised our consciousness that although African-Americans and Spanish-speaking children make up the majority of students in many large urban school districts, the number of black and minority teachers continues to decline. In fact, by the year 2000, the number of African-American teachers will be a mere 5 percent (Garibaldi, 1986), considerably less than the number of African-Americans (12 percent) in the total population. The demographic imbalance that exists between students of color and teachers of color is one that should be taken seriously.

It is important to recruit people of color into teaching (Garibaldi, 1986; Ladson-Billings, 1991). The recruitment issue is important not only for demographic reasons but also for educational purposes, for role-modeling, and for mentoring of students of color. Studies of exemplary teaching have demonstrated that high expectations of students of color can make a difference in helping them to achieve success; additionally, these high expectations can be especially meaningful to the students when they come from someone who is of the same ethnic background (Foster, 1991; Ladson-Billings, 1991; Murrell, 1991).

One of the current realities in education is that the access to a wider variety of careers for minorities has decreased the number who enter teaching. In this environment, incentives of all kinds are necessary to recruit bright, young people from different backgrounds into teaching. Additionally, thought and effort are needed to retain them in the field of education (Foster, 1991; Garibaldi, 1986; Ladson-Billings, 1991).

Students of Color's Perspectives on Schooling

Along with the body of literature that focuses on the classroom teacher, studies have recently appeared that are beginning to document the students' perspective. Some of these investigations deal with broad-based samples of students from different ethnic groups, whereas others tend to be more context-focused and smaller in scope.

Turning to one of the larger studies, Steinberg, Dornbusch, and Brown (1992) surveyed 15,000 high school students from nine different high schools in cities throughout the United States. They considered the variables of parenting practices, family values, and youngsters' beliefs about the linkages between academic school success and their future career rewards. The researchers were concerned about ethnic differences in adolescent achievement and were very aware that many studies indicated that African-Americans "generally earn lower grades, drop out more often, and attain less education that do whites" (Mickelson, 1990, p. 44). They were also aware that Hispanic adolescents did not perform as well as whites in school while Asian-American students performed better in school than whites, African-Americans, and Hispanics.

The researchers uncovered far from simple answers. They found that "adolescents whose parents are warm, firm, and democratic achieve more in school than their peers" (p. 728). At the same time, however, they discovered that parenting style was only part of the picture. Another important factor was the peer group. The differences in the intersection of peer group and parenting seemed to create some very real distinctions among the four ethnic groups studied. In the final analysis, the authors felt that they had a long way to go to explain the phenomenon of ethnic achievement. They advocated the need for more ethnographic studies and for "the ecological approach, with its focus on the multiple contexts in which youngsters live" (p. 729).

Ethnographic Studies of Schools from the Ethnic Perspective

Several ethnographic studies have recently been published that have investigated the phenomenon of ethnic achievement from the students' perspective as well as from the perspective of effective teaching. These investigations have begun to document the ways in which schooling and the culture of people of color affect each other. Culture includes not just parenting and the peer group, it also takes into account ethnic rituals, customs, and peoples' beliefs. This research frequently indicates that the student's culture is often in conflict with the culture in the school. While these ethnographic studies focus on ethnicity, they also include the intersection of ethnicity with social class and gender. They tend to provide rich descriptions of the context of schooling.

For example, very interesting studies can be found that make comparisons between white ethnic groups and African-American groups. In MacLeod's (1987) ethnographic study of "the brothers" and "the hallway hangers," the reader is presented with two sets of young working-class males in an urban environment in the northeastern United States. MacLeod described what he calls the brothers as a group of African-American males who for the most part accepted the middle-class values of the school for success. The author also painted a portrait of the hallway hangers who were predominately white and who believed that schooling would not lead to success in their later lives. Despite their high hopes, the brothers were generally doing only average work academically and were primarily in the vocational track. Although desirous of meeting the school's definition of success, they were not up to the white middle-class standards and faced constant failure. On the other hand, the white working-class group, the hallway hangers, tended to maintain their self-esteem because they did not rely on the school's definition of success. Instead, they looked to wealthy people in the neighborhood, who were often not well educated, to serve as their role models.

The school, according to MacLeod, was not doing its job either for the African-American brothers or the white hallway hangers. Different kinds of interventions were needed for the separate ethnic groups. In the case of the former, skill development and other types of compensatory education were needed; in the latter instance, appropriate role models might make a difference. In MacLeod's study, understanding the attitudes and backgrounds of diverse students, within the context of the school, was essential to determine how to educate each group in the most appropriate ways.

In *Sandbox Society,* Lubeck (1985) compared a white, middle-class preschool with an African-American, lower-class preschool. Lubeck described, in great detail, how teachers worked with the youngsters on the two sites. One such description focused on the language that enabled teachers to communicate with their students within the classroom. For example, at Harmony, the white, middle-class, preschool children were requested to carry out tasks through, what Lubeck called, "indirect directives." A teacher would ask,

> "Would you like to sit in that seat over there?"
> "Would you like to put the salt in the bowl?"
> "Adam, can you put the oil in?" (p. 119)

On the other hand, at Irving Head Start, the African-American lower-class preschool, teachers tended to give explicit directions:

> This is a game: When we go to the restrooms we have to be quiet. If we're not, it will upset other people. The other part of the game is that, if you don't, you're going to get punished for it. You have to have respect for people. (p. 74)

In her discussion, Lubeck indicated that teachers at Harmony Preschool educated white, middle-class youngsters for a society that was made up of predominately nuclear, individualistic families. At the Irving Head Start School, however, what emerged was a pattern of instruction that prepared the black, lower-class youngsters for a community of extended families and of shared values. What is especially positive about this study is that a value judgement was not made to indicate what was the best approach to communication or teaching for the young children in the study (Parker and Shapiro, 1993). Lubeck exhibited a high regard for difference and indicated the importance of accepting, understanding, and respecting diverse ways of communication and varied ways of teaching appropriate to the population being taught.

In Fine's (1989) ethnography of Puerto Rican and African-American students who were predominately working class, one of her major findings dealt with how school administrators were concerned with controlling knowledge and often censored, rather than facilitated, the sharing of students' experiences and ideas. Fine described a process that she called, "silencing," which seemed to occur throughout the school. Although paying lip service to the concept of equal opportunity, in reality, the school administration never really addressed the problems that students faced daily. For example, racism was considered to be a taboo topic by administrators and teachers; it was thought that a discussion of the topic would demoralize the students. Dropping out of school, for instance, could not be discussed in class; it was believed that such a discussion might encourage students to do so (p. 136). Also, the silencing often tended towards fostering behavior alien to the students' cultures. For instance, the African-American and Hispanic students were rewarded for being quiet, obedient, and hard-working. When they displayed more assertive behaviors, some of which were more in keeping with their own cultures at home, they were chastised and told that they would end up on welfare (p. 162). Acceptable cultural standards were those of the white, middle class and not of the cultures from which the majority of the students came. Studies by Au and Jordan (1980), Heath (1982), and Michaels (1981) are just some of those that have indicated the lack of fit between the culture of schooling and the cultures of diverse ethnic groups.

What is clear from many of these studies is that frequently the students of color who manage to succeed in school have had to sacrifice their own culture to do so. They have turned to what Fordham (1988) has described as a pattern of "racelessness." Fordham believes that many high-achieving African-American students have been forced to cling to an imposed and largely false American dream, thereby achieving the individualistic reward of being a winner within the system. In the process, they have had to forfeit much of their own identity and sense of belonging within the African-American community. Fordham (1988), in a thoughtful article, raised some questions for African-American parents that might be worth consideration by other ethnic minority groups as well. She asked,

> (1) Are we willing to have our children defined as successful even though they display very little commitment to the Black community? (2) Or are we more committed to the integrity of the existing cultural system in the Black community and, therefore, willing to sublimate our individual goals for the collective advancement of our people? (p. 81)

Fordham, with the help of LeVine and White (1986), raised another equally important question but this time directed at school administrators and not parents:

> Are you willing to modify existing school curricula to incorporate a more group-centered ethos, thereby enabling Black students to "seek self-realization through personal effort in service to the group?" (p. 81)

Implications of Ethnicity/Race for Education

Teacher educators need to be aware of the work currently being carried out to transform the curriculum in the area of ethnicity/race. Asante (1991–1992) stated this well when he wrote,

> The teacher who teaches American literature and does not refer to the African-American writer is doing a disservice to students of all cultural backgrounds. Equally so, the teacher who teaches music and does not mention one composition by an African-American is de-centering the African-American child and miseducating the rest of the children. (p. 30)

Additionally, Sleeter and Grant (1988) recommended what they called the "single-group approach" to change, such as ethnic differences, as a good starting point to making modifications in the curriculum. By this, they meant that Asante's view or Gomez's parallel focus on Hispanic culture could make a difference to students in a classroom who had previously felt invisible (Sleeter and Grant, 1988, p. 127). By including the accomplishments of people of color, students from different ethnic groups cannot help but feel a certain pride when their culture's works, values, customs, and practices are valued. The hope would be that their achievement in school would rise because at long last what they learned in school would be connected to and extended beyond what they learned at home.

Murrell (1991) has felt that the connections between the culture of the home and the culture of the school have been missing in educational discourse and in the knowledge base of education for far too long. He spoke of the need for teaching and research to be more specifically focused on "experiential knowledge in a social context, particularly as it relates to problematics of race, class, gender, and culture" (p. 206). By this he meant the need for a focus more on "connected knowing" (Belenky et al., 1986) through field-based hands-on projects and, when this is not possible, then through simulated experiences. Connected knowing, or knowledge related to experience, is preferred by many educators to the continued focus on abstract or "separate knowing" that is often too remote for the learner to understand and is too removed from the students' own culture at home.

PART II

Differences in Degree

THE NEXT TWO chapters will present those variables that we have called differences in degree. To parallel our presention in Part I, we have decided to focus Chapter 4 on learning styles since this category of variable is generic and representative of the remaining variables that we will present in this section of the book. Chapter 5 will contain more brief presentations of multiple intelligences, learning disability, and giftedness.

Learning Styles

INTRODUCTION TO LEARNING STYLES

WE WILL BEGIN this section of the book by reviewing the theoretical and empirical literature on learning styles. Similar to our presentation of sex and gender in the previous section of the book, the area of learning styles captures most of the essential issues that characterize those variables that we have termed differences in degree. As before, we will include an extended presentation of learning styles, with somewhat shorter presentations of the other constructs that we have decided to include in this section of the book.

The extensive literature on learning styles is based on the assumption that students enter a learning situation with a variety of skills, preferences, and capacities that affect their learning. Assumably, a learning environment that uses an individual learner' s strengths and is adapted to his or her preferences should facilitate learning for that student. Another student, with different strengths and different preferences, will do better in a different environment. Thus, a student who learns more easily with material presented visually, who prefers working in a small group, and who responds better to bright lighting (to use three examples) would do well academically in an environment that has been modified to contain these three elements. Conversely, a student who learns better using auditory input, who does not work well in groups, and who prefers a less stimulating environment needs a learning environment that matches these characteristics.

Learning style theorists claim that explicit attention to learning styles will improve the educational process in several ways. They argue that the way the curriculum is designed, the type of instructional methods used, and the way learning is assessed can and should be affected by the students' learning styles (Curry, 1990). For example, a classroom that is structured so that the needs of visual learners as well as the needs of auditory learners are met (to use a common example) should be one where student achievement is maximized. In such a classroom, material would be presented using both auditory and visual modalities, classroom exercises would be flexible enough to permit both types of students to use their preferred perceptual styles, and learning would be assessed in a manner that allows all learners to adequately demonstrate what they know. Although there is little disagreement about the general idea that individual differences should be accommodated in the classroom, there is considerable disagreement about many of the specific details in this area. The primary question that remains unresolved is just how much difference it makes if learning styles are taken into account when organizing a learning environment for instruction.

We have chosen to use the term "learning style" rather than the term "cognitive style" [as Corno and Snow (1986) have done] because the focus of the chapter is on instruction and because learning style seems to be the more preferred concept in the educational literature. As Keefe and Ferrell (1990) point out, the two concepts are often confused and the distinctions between them are often blurred. Cognitive style has been used for a longer period of time (Allport, 1924) and these constructs, at least in theory, are prerequisites to learning styles. Although we will focus most of this chapter on learning styles, a brief presentation of one cognitive style variable might serve as an introduction by placing the discussion in a broader context.

An excellent example of a cognitive style that has received considerable attention in the educational literature is field independence/dependence. This construct was defined in the work of Witkin and his associates (1974) as the tendency to approach a situation in an analytic versus a global (or sequential versus wholistic) way. Witkin found in his research that some subjects seemed to have the ability to succeed at tasks with little regard for the surrounding environment, whereas others were dependent on the visual field. He demonstrated this in the classic "rod and frame" test. In this test, subjects are asked to orient a rod vertically despite the orientation of the surrounding frame in which the rod is placed. Field-independent people can do this task at a much higher level than field-dependent individuals. (That is, field-independent subjects can place the rod in a true vertical position regardless of how much the surrounding frame is tilted out of the vertical plane.) Witkin came to believe that this ability reflected a much deeper cognitive processing difference between individuals. In Witkin's theory, field-independent individuals focus on specific information in the environment, learn in an analytical manner, tend to prefer more impersonal relationships and learning environments, and are able to impose structure on chaotic situations. Field-dependent individuals, on the other hand, are more dependent on cues from the environment, are global learners, are good at interpersonal relationships, and prefer to learn material that involves human contact. Of most interest in the present discussion is that these characteristics have been associated with varying degrees of success in school, with the advantage usually belonging to field-independent students.

It should be stressed that Witkin was careful to avoid characterizing either of his cognitive styles as good or bad. Field-independent subjects were viewed as having one set of tendencies, whereas field-dependent subjects possessed other tendencies—both ends of this continuum had advantages and disadvantages. In applying his constructs to a school environment, however, it was usually found that field-independent students achieved at higher levels than field-dependent subjects (Witkin, 1974). In general, the explanation for this phenomenon has focused on the structure of many American classrooms. The typical American classroom is a place where the memorization of facts is stressed, where individual achievement (as opposed to group achievement) is emphasized, where cognition is stressed over affect, and where instruction is linear and hierarchical. All of these characteristics would favor a field-independent learner. To reiterate a point made earlier, Witkin's theory does not lead to a criticism of this because one style is simply viewed as one alternative and one set of strengths is always offset by a set of weaknesses. From the perspective of learning style, however, a problem arises if those students who are field dependent are not given an equal chance to succeed by ensuring that the classroom environment can also meet their unique needs. In an essential way, therefore, all of the arguments that have been raised about field independence/dependence can be raised about any of the learning style variables that we will discuss later in this part of the book.

We have introduced the broad concept of cognitive style and the specific example of field independence/dependence because these constructs are similar to learning styles. Theoretically, the cognitive style of field independence is both broader and more basic than a learning style such as "auditory processing." Many of the other cognitive style variables (e.g., tolerance for ambiguity and locus of control) are assumed to act in essentially the same manner. Basically, however, the pedagogical implications of these variables are identical to the implications of any learning style variable. That is, learning environments should be structured to facilitate the performance of all students because students bring difference needs, strengths, and preferences to these environments.

Reporting on the results of the National Association of Secondary School Principals' (NASSP) task force on learning styles, Keefe and Languis (1983) present a relatively encompassing and theoretically neutral definition. According to these authors, learning styles are,

> The composite of characteristic cognitive, affective, and physiological factors that serve as relatively stable indicators of how a learner perceives, interacts with, and responds to the learning environment. It is demonstrated in that pattern of behavior and performance by which an individual approaches educational experiences. Its basis lies in the structure of neural organization and personality which both molds and is molded by human development and the learning experience of home, school, and society. (p. 59)

The main elements of the above definition—the cognitive, affective, and physiological aspects of learning styles and their derivation from both innate (i.e., genetic) and learned (i.e., cultural) sources—allows the authors to straddle most of the thornier issues in this area. In fact, considerable controversy exists about the exact nature of learning styles and about their cause. Of the three comprehensive models of learning style that exist (Dunn, Dunn, and Price, 1975, 1979, 1981, 1985; Hill, 1971; Keefe and Monk, 1986), all assume to some extent that there are significant physiological underpinnings to learning styles, with the Dunns having set forward a fairly elaborate theory linking learning styles to right and left cerebral dominance (Dunn, Beudry, and Klavas, 1989). On the other hand, writers who are more concerned about cultural influences on learning styles either downplay or deny their physiological basis [see, for example, Shade (1989) and Hernandez (1989)].

HOW MANY LEARNING STYLES?

Although there is some agreement about the essential categories of learning styles (almost all writers, for example, include at least one style that is similar to the analytic/global distinction made in field-independence research), there is little agreement about the exact number of learning style variables or what specific learning styles exist. The work of Dunn et al. (1975), for example, yields twenty-one styles that are classified into five broad groupings: environmental factors, emotional factors, sociological preferences, physiological needs, and cognitive-psychological inclinations. Table 4.1, again taken from the work of the NASSP task force (1983), presents a fairly representative list of learning styles.

It is evident from Table 4.1 that a wide range of variables is included that covers almost all aspects of the learner/environment interaction. It is also evident that the list in Table 4.1 includes styles that differ widely in generalizability and importance, characteristics that almost all of the learning style theories share.

PERSISTENT ISSUES IN LEARNING STYLES

As we have mentioned, the basic idea that individuals differ and that instruction should be modified to take these individual differences into

Table 4.1 *A Listing of Learning Styles.*

A. Perceptual Styles
1. Visual—initial reaction to information is visual
2. Auditory—initial reaction to information is auditory
3. Emotive—initial reaction to information is emotive

B. Cognitive Styles
4. Analytic—identifies critical elements of a problem
5. Spatial—identifies shapes and objects in mental space
6. Discrimination—visualize important elements of task
7. Categorization—use of reasonable criteria for classifying information
8. Sequential processing—process information sequentially
9. Simultaneous processing—process information visuospatially
10. Memory—ability to retain information
11. Verbal—spatial preference—choice of verbal or nonverbal
12. Persistence—willingness to work until completed
13. Verbal risk—willingness to express opinions
14. Manipulative—desire for "hands-on" activities
15. Study time preference (early morning)
16. Study time preference (late morning)
17. Study time preference (afternoon)
18. Study time preference (evening)
19. Grouping preference—desire to learn in a whole class vs. dyadic groupings
20. Posture preference—desire for formal vs. informal study
21. Mobility preference—desire for taking breaks while studying
22. Sound preference—desire to study in quiet vs. study with background sound
23. Lighting preference—desire for bright or lower lighting
24. Temperature preference—desire for cool or warm environments

account is not controversial as a general premise. The specific way this is accomplished, however, has produced several continuing controversies in this area. Curry (1990) lists three general problems that she perceives: 1) confusion in definitions; 2) weakness in the assessment instruments; and 3) inconclusive results from research involving the matching of learner characteristics and learning environments. Because we have already reviewed some of the issues regarding the definition of learning style, we will briefly comment on the other two issues and will then review the topic of cultural, racial, and linguistic differences in learning style.

Issues Regarding the Assessment Instruments

There are several widely used learning style batteries, with those by Dunn, Dunn, and Price (1975) (the Learning Style Questionnaire), Carbo (1981) (the Reading Style Inventory), and Keefe et al. (1986) (the Learning Style Profile) being three of the most common. In general, all of the existing batteries assess a variety of learning styles and produce a profile of an individual learner's strengths and weaknesses (or strong and weak preferences depending on the focus of the learning style theory). Evidence for the reliability of these scales varies from strong to marginal (internal consistency measures, for example, range from .3 to .9 using Cronbach's Alpha; test-retest reliabilities, where available, range from .2 to .7 over periods of time ranging from two weeks to more than two months).

The evidence for validity is a more complex issue, due largely to the fact that the field has not reached a consensus about what should and should not be correlated with learning styles. Given this situation, it is difficult, if not impossible, to make firm statements about the construct validity of any of the batteries. At best, what can be done at this time is to review the evidence by the authors of the scales and judge from these presentations how adequate the scales seem to be. [See Dunn, Beaudry, and Klavas (1989) and Keefe and Ferrell (1990), for reviews of research on two of the scales.]

Issues Regarding the Matching of Learners and Learning Environments

The critical test of learning style theory is to show that students perform better in learning environments that are matched to their learning style. An ideal research design would create a variety of learning environments structured around major learning styles and would then assign students to these environments so that their learning style matches or does not match the environment. Although there is a considerable body of research of this type, a fair generalization of this research is that the evidence is contradictory. As reviewed by Curry (1990), there are about as many studies that show a positive matching effect (e.g., Douglas, 1979; Steele, 1986; Tannenbaum, 1982) as there are studies that show no effect (Cholakis, 1986; DeGregoris, 1986; Stiles, 1985). Moreover, there are some studies that show that students who are mismatched do better than those who are matched appropriately (Kirby, 1988; Knight, 1990).

Perhaps the most telling criticism of the matching assumption comes from the work of Cohen et al. (1989). In a detailed analysis of the learning style research, these authors found that almost all of the studies demonstrating a positive effect for learning style matching occurred in studies where the instruction was precisely defined, the outcomes were clearly detailed, and both instructors and students knew how the instruction and assessment were aligned. In other words, the treatment produced a positive effect on achievement not because the instruction and the learning style were matched, but rather because the research forced the teachers to be clear and coherent in their instruction.

Are There Cultural or Racial Differences in Learning Style?

The final issue we wish to review is the topic of cultural or racial differences in learning style. While many of these writings have focused on African-Americans, some more recent research has included Latino and Asian students. In general, researchers in this area have attempted to demonstrate that certain cultural or racial groups demonstrate a consistent pattern of learning styles, which is different from the pattern demonstrated by other groups. Both Carbo, Dunn, and Dunn (1986) and Hale-Benson (1982), for example, have discussed the "black learning style" and have characterized it as being "global, holistic, simultaneous, and field-dependent" (Dunn et al., 1990). The issue of an African-American learning style has also been raised by Shade (1982, 1986) who argues that the culturally induced focus on people and social interactions rather than products or individual achievement in African-American students may be one of the causes of their lower levels of achievement in school. In a more recent and data-based article, Dunn et al. (1990) compared the learning styles of African-American, Chinese-American, Greek-American, and Mexican-American children. These authors found statistically significant differences between the groups, although in some cases the groups were more similar than dissimilar on certain learning style variables. Similar findings have been reported by Jalali (1989) who found distinct patterns of preferences among six different racial groups. African-American students, for example, preferred learning under conditions that were quiet, warm, bright, routine, and contained feedback from an authority figure. Mexican-Americans, on the other hand, preferred low light, high structure, and learning alone, although they were similar to African-Americans in preferring to receive feedback from an authority figure.

As is true in many areas of learning style research and theory, the issue of consistent differences between racial or cultural groups is confusing and unclear. As is so often the case, the theoretical writing is much stronger than the data base that supports it. Moreover, in any discussion of racial or cultural differences, the effects of social class and/or ethnicity must be taken into account. As we have already mentioned in this book, the overlapping effects of race, ethnicity, and social class are complex. Because most of the research that has attempted to find racial differences in learning style has not adequately accounted for these overlapping and interactive effects, the existence of racial or cultural differences that are important enough to be considered in planning instruction must remain an open question.

LANGUAGE DIVERSITY AND LEARNING STYLES

> The language of this classroom is English. This is America. We will only speak English in class and on the school grounds. (Candelaria, 1993, p. 118)

We have decided to introduce language diversity at this point in the book because some of the critical issues in this complex area are discussed in the literature under the general rubric of learning styles. Obviously, language differences are not merely differences in learning style. In fact, many writers equate language with culture and call students who speak languages other than English "culturally/linguistically diverse" (Garcia, 1993). As the quotation cited above indicates, however, linguistic diversity is no less an issue in American classrooms than are any of the other aspects of difference that are mentioned throughout this book. Because of the complexity of this topic, we have decided to present only a brief overview of some of the central issues and then focus on linguistic diversity as a reflection of learning styles.

Because of current immigration patterns, schools in the United States are increasingly becoming centers of diverse languages. As of 1987, for example, students in the Los Angeles school district spoke seventy-nine languages and the district offered bilingual instruction in Spanish, Cantonese, Vietnamese, Korean, Filipino, and Armenian (Ovando, 1989). For the United States as a whole, the decade of the 1980s produced considerable growth in language diversity. During that period, Hispanics increased by 61 percent and Asian-Americans by 141 percent (Banks, 1991; Cortes, 1986). As Garcia (1993) points out, in less than forty years, white, non-Hispanic students will be a minority in every category of public education as we know it today. This group of ethnically and racially diverse students, the "emerging majority" to use Garcia's term, will dominate American public education well into the 21st century.

Previously, teachers felt it was appropriate to say that they required English-only in their classrooms, as in the quotation at the beginning of this section. However, during the 1970s and 1980s, with the striking growth of language diversity and with the increasing awareness of diversity, legislation offering more equitable treatment of limited-English-proficient (LEP) students made its appearance. Both the 1986 Title VII Bilingual Education Act and the important U.S. Supreme Court Decision of *Lau* vs. *Nichols* (1974) offered legal foundations for fairness towards LEP students in schools. However, as with so many laws, legislation could not mandate more positive attitudes towards those who did not speak standard English well nor did it mean that overnight educators would become knowledgeable about how to teach LEP students.

Garcia (1993) argues that there are basically four positions that underlie the research in the area of linguistically and culturally diverse students. Some of these frameworks conceptualize linguistic diversity as an example of cultural diversity (or, to use our distinction, which conceptualize this area as representing a difference in kind), whereas others focus more on learning diversity or differences in degree. We will briefly present these four positions, and we refer the reader to the original reference for a more complete presentation.

The first position that Garcia describes is really not a position that stems from the perspective of diversity as we have written about it in this book. Rather, this position argues that there are robust pedagogical principles that work for all learners (or, to weaken this a bit, for almost all learners) in all contexts. This framework comes from the works of Walberg (1986) and Wang, Haertel, and Walberg (1993). Their research focuses on metanalysis and identifying effective educational techniques that work across all languages and cultures. Such strategies as direct instruction (Rosenshine and Stevens, 1986), tutoring (Bloom, 1984), and cooperative learning (Slavin and Madden, 1989) have been frequently cited by authors from this framework as effective techniques for all students no matter what their home backgrounds may be.

Another framework, more aligned to the concept of diversity, argues that "linguistic and culturally diverse populations call for deeper understanding of the interaction of students' home cultures and languages and the prevailing school culture and language" (Tharpe, 1989). A large body of ethnographic research, crossing different cultures, supports this argument, including the studies of Ada (1988), Heath (1983), and Wiesner, Gallimore, and Jordan (1988), to name but a few. These studies tend to describe a clash of the home and school cultures that can cause considerable difficulties for students attempting to learn English and trying to fit into the American mainstream. This framework posits that using the student's home language and cultural supports within the school can make for a more positive learning environment (August and Garcia, 1988; Wong-Fillmore, 1991) and can therefore improve achievement for LEP students.

A third framework, discussed by Garcia (1993), emanates from the work of Freire (1970) and is further expanded by Cummins (1986) and Pearl (1991). This concept indicates that no matter what the intervention strategy or modification within the school, if the social circumstances remain oppressive, the pedagogy could be tainted. These writers speak of pedagogy that must be empowering and activist in nature for change to occur.

Finally, a fourth framework comes primarily out of the work of Ogbu (1987a,b) which looks at society from a caste perspective. Ogbu indicates that too many classrooms are characterized by the expectation that certain people are not meant to achieve. This expectation affects the way students who are characterized in a negative manner are taught. Unless expectations rise, there is virtually no hope that the majority of students perceived to be in a lower caste will be given a proper opportunity to learn.

Each of these frameworks has an effect on how students are treated in school and what is expected of them. However, the frameworks can overlap adding even more complexity to the area of linguistically and culturally diverse students. As Garcia comments,

> These approaches suggest that the underachievement of linguistically and culturally diverse students can be attributed to a number of complex interrelationships among society, the home, and the school itself. Even more precisely, the focus sharpens the examination of language and culture embodied by parents/caretakers, siblings, and peers in the home and community and teachers, peers, and administrators in the classroom and school. (p. 56)

Despite the differences in the frameworks and moving from more of a theoretical level to one of practice, there are some things we know about how students learn another language. For example, Torrey (1983) has emphasized that the home dialect is important. In this regard, her concept of a learning style or pedagogical approach

> affirms the importance of home dialect and its appropriate use within the community in which it is spoken while at the same time students are taught the standard variety. Affirming home language means that students may produce utterances in the classroom in native dialect without being told that they are wrong or that what they say is vulgar or bad. Instead, the teacher analyzes with the students the differences between their dialect and the standard variety: grammatical patterns, pronunciation, vocabulary items, varying social contexts, and so on. (p. 627)

However, Torrey's concept of language acquisition is not the only one in the literature. After more than a decade and a half of work with young children for whom English is a second language, Wong-Fillmore (1991) has developed an emerging model of language learning. Within her model, there are three major components. They include: "(1) learners who realize that they need to learn the target language (T.L.) and are motivated to do so; (2) speakers of the target language who know it well enough to provide the learners with access to the language and the help they need for learning it; and (3) a social setting which brings learners and T.L. speakers into frequent enough contact to make language learning possible" (pp. 52–53). In this model, Wong-Fillmore advocates a direct instructional style rather than a cooperative learning approach and emphasizes the importance of interactions for the learner enabling the person to try out the language in a supportive and yet a corrective atmosphere. Her concept is one of student-centeredness up to a point; however, she believes it does the student a disservice if the teaching is not sufficiently demanding ensuring that the student will begin to fit into the new culture.

Wong-Fillmore (1991) stresses that there is much variation in how a second-language learner learns. She writes, "Learners who have poor auditory memory will have a difficult time remembering the things they hear in a new language. If they cannot remember what they hear, they will not find it easy to figure out what it means or how it is structured" (p. 61). Not only does the learner vary considerably, but classrooms also vary considerably as well. Within the classrooms, in her model, those teaching the T.L. must know the language well enough to provide reliable samples of it for the learners to work on. Additionally, the attitudes and beliefs of the T.L. speakers can affect the amount of language learning that takes place. Despite the variations of the students and their classrooms, Wong-Fillmore has found that "when there are regular activities that both invite and support the use of the target language in the context of learning about subject matter that is made relevant and interesting to the children, they learn the language, with or without much additional informal social contact with speakers" (p. 65).

Macias' (1989) and Schuhmann's (1992) writings about language acquisition has focused more on the preparation of teachers to work with LEP students than on the students themselves by stressing the concept of a paradigm shift. By this, both Macias and Schuhmann meant that teachers needed to believe "that language-minority students can and will learn, and that the use of non-English languages is not un-American" (Schuhmann, 1992, p. 107).

LINGUISTIC DIVERSITY AND LEARNING STYLE

As we mentioned at the beginning of this section, the area of linguistic diversity is complex and encompasses a variety of issues. For example, there is a continuing debate focusing on the education of culturally and linguistically diverse students in the United States with special attention to the instructional use of the native language instead of, or in addition to, English. At one end of the spectrum are the "supporters of native language instruction" (Garcia, 1993, p. 77). Supporters of this approach favor the use of the student's native language and mastery of that language prior to the introduction of an English curriculum. In this case, the native language is meant to provide important cognitive and social foundations for second-language learning. ''At the other end of the debate, introduction of the English curriculum is recommended at the onset of the student's schooling experience with minimal use of the native language'' (Garcia, 1993, p. 77). There are also debates about how much the curriculum should reflect the cultural background of the students in the class (for example, by introducing role models from other cultures in addition to the traditional role models that have characterized the curriculum of American schools), and whether linguistically diverse students require different assessment strategies than speakers of English.

The issue we wish to address in this part of the book is whether language differences reflect differences in learning style. Using the field independence/dependence construct introduced earlier, many writers have noted that the dominant middle-class value system in the United States is characterized by individual attainment of goals (as contrasted to group attainment), independence, self-sufficiency, autonomy, and competitiveness. All of these can be defined as critical aspects of field independence. As a reflection of this value system, American schools and classrooms reinforce and reward students who perform in accordance with these values. What, then, of students whose culture does not reinforce or reward these values? What will happen to students who have been taught by their home and their culture that interdependence is valued, that competitiveness is wrong and that individual achievement should be subjugated to group accomplishment? Will these field-dependent students perform as well as students who more closely fit the culture of the classroom?

Arguments such as these are at the center of the discussion of linguistic diversity viewed through the lens of learning style. We have focused our presentation on field independence/dependence, although exactly the same argument can and has been made about other variables. The research by Jalali (1989), which we cited earlier, looked at a range of learning style variables such as auditory versus visual processing, tactile preferences, afternoon versus morning learning, etc. as a function of the student's ethnic group. The general point that these researchers are trying to make is that groups of students who differ in their linguistic and/or cultural background can sometimes also be characterized by more or less distinct patterns of learning styles. If, as is so often the case, this pattern is discrepant from the middle-class norm that typifies the usual American classroom, these students will be at a disadvantage in that classroom.

SUMMARY: THE IMPLICATIONS OF LEARNING STYLES FOR EDUCATION

It is quite clear that teacher educators should understand the essential rationale underlying the call for environments that are sensitive and appropriate for individual learners. If nothing else, instruction at all levels should use varied formats and modalities, and some general matching of a student's strengths and preferences with instruction should be employed. To the extent that learning style theorists have furthered this general idea in education, they have had a positive effect. There are, however, some words of caution.

One of the disadvantages of the linkage of racial, cultural, or linguistic groupings to learning styles is that such thinking can lead to treating all members of a specific group as if they belonged to an undifferentiated whole. It is surely as wrong to assume that all African-Americans or all Hispanic-Americans are the same as it is to assume that all middle-class, white Americans are the same. Even if reliable between-group variation in learning style can be found, there will always be enough within-group variation to make simple statements about any member of the group problematic. Moreover, individuals are capable of modification and change, and new learning styles, or modifications in existing learning styles, can be suggested. Just as it is wrong to assume that a given individual's IQ sets nonmodifiable limits on his or her ability to learn, so it is wrong to assume that an individual's cultural or linguistic background causes the individual to perceive or act in a way that must remain constant throughout the individual's life.

In addition to the problem of assuming that class membership explains too much, there is also the problem that the proponents of learning styles have been a bit too aggressive in proselytizing their theory. In general, the specific claims of these theorists, and particularly the amount of advocacy for their positions, seem unwarranted or at least exaggerated. At the present time, learning style theory represents more of a promise than a reality for educational practice. What is clear, however, is that people learn differently and that some learners have strengths in areas that are unique to them and that make them different from other learners (visual learners versus auditory learners; analytic problem solvers versus global problem solvers, etc). It is a truism to assert that this general idea needs to be taken into account by educators, and the proponents of learning styles have fostered this general notion better than any other group.

CHAPTER 5

Other Aspects of Diversity Viewed as Differences in Degree

MULTIPLE INTELLIGENCES

Introduction to Multiple Intelligences

WE WILL BEGIN our presentation of the other aspects of diversity, which we have termed differences in degree, with a review of multiple intelligences. Like learning styles, this construct shares many of the essential characteristics of current thinking on the topic of diversity. In particular, the literature in this area demonstrates one of the most notable shifts in educational thinking in recent years: the movement from a unitary and simpler concept of ability to a multivariate and more complex concept. Although the conception of intelligence associated with multiple intelligences is neither entirely original nor entirely new, its emphasis on the pluralistic notion of intelligence and on an individual's ability to develop valuable products in one or more cultural settings is particularly relevant to this chapter's focus on issues of diversity in general, and ethnicity, social class, and gender in particular.

A complete understanding of multiple intelligences would entail a lengthy presentation of several critical issues. These would include: 1) an historical and theoretical discussion of the development of intelligence tests; 2) a presentation of the literature that has argued for the biological bases of intelligence coupled with the often opposing literature, which argues that intellectual competencies can be trained (a controversy which helps to explain the recent furor over *The Bell Curve* by Hernstein and Murray (1994); and 3) the implications for the assessment of intelligence in children from different social classes or from ethnically diverse backgrounds. Obviously, the limited space available to each of the constructs in this chapter precludes an in-depth presentation on any of these topics. We will, however, attempt a brief presentation of some background concepts to place the discussion in a historical context.

Theories of Intelligence

First conceived by the French psychologist, Alfred Binet, the original intelligence test was commissioned by the French government as a selection device to choose students for appropriate levels of instruction within schools. As such, the 1905 Binet test was designed to determine a child's level of intellectual competence as a basis for effective teaching and remediation. It was when Binet's test was brought to America, however, that the concept of intelligence as we presently know it began to take shape. From its very inception in American society, the atheoretical, practical instrument of Binet was transformed and expanded into a tool with far-reaching implications for American education. Legitimized by the expanding science of psychology, the Binet test and the theoretical structure that was devised to validate its use became the basis for a political philosophy marked by a distinction between different racial, ethnic, and cultural groups (Terman, 1916).

This shift in purpose, from helping children with learning difficulties to identifying and labelling children as uneducable (Schiff and Lewontin, 1986), corresponded to the development of theories of intelligence that served as the theoretical justification for the multifaceted uses of intelligence tests. Among the most influential early scientific contributions to the theoretical underpinning of testing instruments were the "general intelligence" theory of Spearman (1927) and the equally influential "primary mental abilities" theory of Thurstone (1938). Framing the Spearman and Thurstone theories in the context of a geographic model depicted as a "map of the mind," Sternberg (1988) points to the emphasis on general intelligence as a major region of the mind in Spearman's model. In contrast, Thurstone discounted the notion of a single major region of the mind and instead identified seven major regions. According to Thurstone, the abilities associated with these regions were: verbal comprehension, verbal fluency, inductive reasoning, spatial visualization, perceptual speed, number, and memory.

General Intelligence versus Several Intelligences

It is in the context of this debate between a unitary concept of intelligence and the idea of several intelligences that Howard Gardner

(1983) placed his theory of multiple intelligences (MI). At the core of the MI theory is the fundamental belief in the existence of different intellectual strengths and competencies. If, as Gardner and his associates argue (Gardner, 1983; Gardner and Hatch, 1989; Walters and Gardner, 1986), these intellectual competencies can be identified in the manifestation of valued activities in a given cultural setting, the MI theory stands in sharp contrast to the notion of general intelligence or a single unitary ability. To understand this conceptual difference, one must not only examine what constitutes intelligence from different theoretical perspectives but also, more importantly, how the conception of intelligence evolves.

Gardner arrived at seven intellectual competencies by investigating the criteria or signs of intelligence from a variety of sources. These included: studies of normal development; information from neuropsychology, particularly the cognitive functioning of brain-damaged individuals; studies of exceptional individuals and the existence of idiot savants and prodigies; empirical findings from psychometric studies, and support from cross-cultural research. The inclusion of expert end-state performance in adults among the criteria for the definition of intelligence is an important distinguishing characteristic of the MI theory, particularly relevant to the issue of fairness in the assessment of culturally diverse populations.

The seven intelligences outlined in Gardner's *Frames of the Mind* (1983) are:

(*1*) *Linguistic Intelligence:* Verbal ability has been a core component of intelligence from its earliest conception and measurement. It also emerges from the various sources providing the criteria for intelligence as a defensible component. Language skills demonstrated in poets and other writers assure an ability to deal with verbal symbols and the various functions of language.

(*2*) *Logical-Mathematical Intelligence:* This form of intelligence is exemplified by the ability to manipulate mathematical and scientific symbols. The emphasis on the ability to use logical and numerical skills to handle a long chain of reasoning is also fundamental to traditional conceptions of intelligence.

(*3*) *Musical Intelligence:* Biological underpinning has been invoked to suggest that musical expressiveness passes the criteria to be identified as a particular intelligence. Moreover, musical skills yield highly valued cultural products, thus meeting a criterion for consideration. The accomplishments of musical prodigies either through natural talent or by education are remarkable demonstrations of intellectual competence.

(4) *Spatial Intelligence:* The expert performances of navigators and architects are reflective of spatial abilities. It is the visual-spatial ability to manipulate or mentally rotate an object to transform it from its original structure.

(5) *Interpersonal Intelligence:* The ability to understand the behavior of humans in complex social environments is often indicative of the intellectual competence observed in salespeople and therapists.

(6) *Bodily Kinesthetic Intelligence:* This is the ability demonstrated by athletes and dancers and indicates the skill with which one is able to control bodily movements.

(7) *Intrapersonal Intelligence:* Self-awareness and self-knowledge are the salient features of intrapersonal intelligence. It is, however, the ability to capitalize on the understanding of one's self-knowledge to guide one's own behavior that constitutes competence.

If, as Gardner argues, these seven intelligences are fundamentally independent of each other, the notion of a single global measure of intelligence as reflected in the traditional IQ score is of questionable merit. To the proponents of the MI theory, the standardized IQ measure, based on weak psychometric support and questionable theories about human functioning, is inadequate to assess the range of human abilities. Furthermore, many culturally meaningful activities such as composing and dancing require different intelligences, which cannot be adequately assessed by IQ tests. A central point in Gardner's formulations is the fundamental shift from conventional tests in which verbal and mathematical abilities are core components of a single measure of intelligence. Gardner argues that only by combining abilities can cultural roles be executed competently.

Assessment of Intelligence: IQ Tests versus Non-IQ Measures

The psychometric, theoretical, and empirical rationale for the validity and practical utility of the IQ test is firmly entrenched in American psychology and education. Its development and theoretical justification have been acknowledged by several of the most gifted psychologists as one of the most fundamental accomplishments in psychology. It is, therefore, quite paradoxical that the theory of multiple intelligences, despite its radical departure from the conception of intelligence underlying IQ tests, has been receiving such favorable attention.

This paradox is cogently presented by Sternberg (1992). If market considerations drive the testing industry as Sternberg implies, it is remarkable that Gardner's conceptualizations are taken seriously when such key school-related demands as accountability, prediction, diagnosis, and placement are apparently not factored into MI's theoretical formulations. Sternberg (1992) has generated a list of what an imaginative test developer might perceive to be the needs of school-based consumers of intelligence tests. Among the various needs are: predicting achievement; high correlations with other, similar tests; ease of administration and interpretation; and objectivity of scoring and perceived fairness. Given the consistency between the perceived consumer needs and the purposes for which the IQ test claims validity, the preeminent role of the IQ test seems clearly established.

If, however, the quality of educational programming becomes the conceptual basis for testing, then there will inevitably be a conflict between the scientific purity of the classic psychometric tradition and the real-life needs of practitioners (Sewell, 1979, 1987). Gardner and his colleagues, instead of following the historical context of testing, have radically shifted the paradigm for the assessment of intelligence. Two central characteristics of their model are worth noting: 1) the model relies heavily on resources from curriculum activities over an extended time period to assess problem-solving skills and to evaluate the ability to fashion products of value; and 2) authentic assessment practices, such as portfolio reviews, are extensively used to measure competence.

Culturally Biased Testing versus Intelligence-Fair Testing

A fundamental principle underlying the assessment process is the requirement that tests should be selected that are not racially or culturally discriminatory. Nevertheless, the literature on IQ testing is replete with inferences of cultural bias (Mensh and Mensh, 1991; Schiff and Lewontin, 1986), litigations based on charges of discriminatory practices (Elliott, 1986), and systematic documentation of adverse social and economical consequences (Gould, 1981; Karmin, 1974). Because American education must be concerned with the education of an increasingly diverse student population, the challenge of either modifying traditional assessment practices or exploring alternative strategies becomes critical. Presumably, based on the existence of seven relatively independent intelligences, the proponents of multiple intelligences will point to the potential of MI theory to assess a wider and more diverse range of human ability. Furthermore, expanding the purpose of testing from the primary historical function of predicting achievement to the use of assessment to identify competencies that are important in everyday life, has substantially increased the potential for "intelligence-fair" assessment. If the basic tenet of autonomous intelligences is correct, and if valid assessment procedures emerge to identify these intellectual competencies without resorting to the narrow focus on mathematical and linguistic skills, the potential to assess children from diverse cultures to meet the range of their human potential seems promising.

Implications of Multiple Intelligence Theory for Education

Much of the highly acclaimed contribution of psychology to education centers around the uses of intelligence tests in schools. But despite the impressive scientific and technical qualities associated with the psychometric tradition in testing, evidence has been accumulating for some time to indicate that the IQ test is not an unbiased index of learning ability or relevant real-world competencies. This serious concern is further exacerbated when attention turns to individuals from low socioeconomic and minority backgrounds. The theory of multiple intelligences has challenged the psychometric paradigm and proposed the existence of intellectual competencies that have been grossly neglected by schools. By proposing a contextual approach to assessment (Kornhaber, Krechevsky, and Gardner, 1990), the MI theory has provided fresh thinking to support the focus on competencies applicable to practical, external world experiences.

It is perhaps the sensitivity of the MI theory to abilities reflected in neglected areas of schooling such as musical ability, interpersonal and intrapersonal social intelligence, and bodily kinesthetic skills that will provide the impetus for schools to nurture culturally meaningful activities. In the context of this book on diversity, the MI theory provides a defensible rationale and offers a realistic possibility that schools will be better able to recognize talents in individuals whose cultural experiences make them different from the white, middle-class student on whom so much educational practice has been based.

LEARNING DISABILITY AND GIFTEDNESS

It is estimated that approximately one out of every six children in a typical classroom can be classified as "exceptional" as this term is used in the educational literature (U.S. Department of Education, 1990). Table 5.1 presents a listing of characteristics commonly defined as exceptional, and gives the approximate incidence in the American population.

As Gage and Berliner (1991) point out, within the American school population of approximately 45 million students, the above estimates would indicate that about 6.5 million children would be considered exceptional. Clearly, this form of diversity is one that all teachers will encounter, especially in light of the mandate through public law 94-142 to place all students in the least restrictive environment. Because the topic of exceptionality is extremely broad and complex, in this chapter we will focus on only those issues that we feel are central to our main topic. Specifically, we will focus our discussion on learning disability and on giftedness, not only because these are the two most prevalent aspects of exceptionalities, but also because most of the critical issues in this area can be discussed in reference to these topics. [The reader is referred to Reynolds' chapter in the AACTE handbook (1988) for a comprehensive discussion of the major topics in this area.]

Learning Disability

All students, even the brightest ones, have difficulty learning some material some of the time. When a student who usually does well in

Table 5.1

Type of Exceptionality	% Incidence in Population
Learning disabled	5.0%
Gifted and talented	4.2%
Speech impaired	2.5%
Mentally retarded	1.4%
Emotionally disturbed	1.0%
Hard of hearing and deaf	.14%
Orthopedically impaired	.12%
Other health impaired	.11%
Multihandicapped	.07%
Visually handicapped	.06%

From Gage and Berliner, 1991, p. 200.

school is having trouble, the source for this difficulty is typically sought in such short-term, controllable causes as a temporary illness, lack of interest in the specific topic, or overcommitment in other areas. There are students, however, who consistently have trouble learning, yet have no obvious reason for this difficulty. If such a problem persists for a period of time, the student could eventually be classified as learning disabled. As is true of many areas of diversity, there is little disagreement about the general premise that learning disabilities exist. The problem, as usual, is in the specifics.

One of the major controversies in the area of learning disabilities concerns the correct definition of this condition. In his recent article, Hammill (1990) reviews eleven different definitions of learning disability, citing the similarities and dissimilarities among them. His preferred definition is reproduced below.

> Learning disabilities is a general term that refers to a heterogeneous group of disorders manifested by significant difficulties in the acquisition and use of listening, speaking, reading, writing, reasoning, or mathematical abilities. These disorders are intrinsic to the individual, presumed to be due to central nervous system dysfunction, and may occur across the life span. Problems in self-regulatory behaviors, social perception, and social interaction may exist with learning disabilities but do not by themselves constitute a learning disability. Although learning disabilities may occur concomitantly with other handicapping conditions (for example, sensory impairment, mental retardation, serious emotional disturbance) or with extrinsic influences (such as cultural differences, insufficient or inappropriate instruction) they are not the results of those conditions or influences. (NJCLD, 1988, p. 1)

As Hammill mentions, the one commonality that all definitions share is the notion that a learning disabled student is an underachiever. In general, this underachievement is defined as either a discrepancy between different achievement domains (e.g., math versus reading) or between a measure of ability, such as an IQ score, and achievement. Moreover, most of the definitions of learning disability exclude a variety of factors (economic and cultural differences, low motivation, poor instruction) as contributing to or causing the condition. Finally, there is a growing consensus that the problem is somehow related to central nervous system functioning, although how and why this occurs is both unclear and controversial.

The second major topic in learning disability concerns the correct instructional approaches that teachers should use to help these students achieve their maximum potential. There is growing literature on this subject focusing on classroom practices as well as on training in areas such as increasing problem solving abilities, decreasing impulsivity, and improving peer relationships [see Lerner (1981) for an early review of this area]. Gage and Berliner (1991) present a series of actions that teachers can use to help deal with the learning disabled in the classroom. These involve a careful observation of the student in various contexts, a comparison of the student with other students to ascertain how atypical the target student's behavior is, a series of steps to determine if the student should be referred for possible special education classification, and some suggestions for developing and implementing an individualized educational plan for the student. The general assumption in most of this literature is that the learning disabled student will be a part of the regular classroom, and that it is the responsibility of the teacher to adapt his or her instruction to this form of diversity.

The Growing Prevalence of Learning Disability

The learning disabled are the fastest growing group of exceptional children in American schools. This rate of increase is evidenced by the following statistics: In 1970, the number of children classified as learning disabled was approximately 150,000; by 1990, the number had increased to 2 million (Gage and Berliner, 1991; Ysseldyke and Algozzine, 1983). It is also interesting that a majority of students who are classified as learning disabled are males. Lerner (1981) for example, estimates that there are four to six times as many males as females classified as learning disabled. Because there is no reason to assume that the actual incidence of this condition has increased to the extent noted above, the growing use of the term learning disabled is striking testimony to the political and social forces that affect the classification and treatment of exceptional children. Special education (to place the discussion in a broader arena) has always been an area open to competing political forces as society struggles with both the definition and the treatment of children who are viewed as deviant. In an earlier time, a far greater percentage of children were classified as mentally defective, based on either poor school performance, low IQ scores, or both. With the increasing attacks on the traditional IQ test and the growing awareness that a disproportionate number of minority and low-SES children were classified as mentally defective, this label has become increasingly unacceptable. The great advantage with the concept of learning disability is that the construct, by definition, excludes many of the factors (e.g., cultural differences) that are known to produce those characteristics that have been previously labelled as mental retardation. It should be emphasized that the school-related manifestations of the condition, such as low achievement or lack of attention in class, have not changed. Rather, what has altered is the cause that is believed to produce these behaviors. Furthermore, by placing the etiology in the domain of central nervous system dysfunctioning, even though the specific action and location are largely unknown, the locus of responsibility for academic failure is shifted away from agents such as parents, teachers, and the school and toward an uncontrollable and unavoidable genetic cause.

All of these factors combine to indicate why learning disability is the classification of choice for the 1990s and why the topic is central to a discussion of diversity in education. By reclassifying a significant number of students who are not achieving at acceptable levels as learning disabled, a category has been created by which these students can be conveniently grouped and treated as a homogeneous subset of students within a classroom. More important, because writers in this field have carefully excluded such factors as cultural differences or poor academic preparation, charges of racial or ethnic bias or of poor teaching, cannot be made. Unlike the mentally retarded, the learning disabled are not intellectually deficient; they do not necessarily have low IQ's; nor are they incapable of learning. To push this argument to its logical conclusion, the existence of the construct learning disability creates for education a politically correct category to put many of its failures, without the necessity of assigning blame to anyone for these failures.

It is not our intent to discredit the general concept of learning disability since underachievement should be a concern of any teacher. Concerns can be raised, however, about the seemingly inevitable tendency to "medicalize" constructs such as learning disability and to transform them into something more closely resembling an illness. For example, there is a clear relationship between learning disability and the diagnostic classification termed "attention deficit hyperactivity disorder" (ADHD) (Robins, 1992; Rutter, 1989). While this topic is too complex to be covered here, it is interesting to note the movement that seems to be occurring from the general construct of learning disability to the specific, medical syndrome of ADHD. Since ADHD is often treated by medication (Ritalin or its generic name of methylphenidate) (Balthazor, Wagner, and Pelham, 1991), the trend we noted above to remediate the problem of underachievement through medical means becomes more evident. Some of this movement is undoubtedly warranted, and some of the medical recommendations being made about a growing number of children are correct. The question that education must face is whether this trend has gone too far and whether the medical profession is the proper location for remediating an increasing number of educational problems.

Implications for Education

Our intent in this section is to point out that achievement, like any other student characteristic, is an aspect of diversity. Not all students achieve at the same level or at the same rate, and most students have areas of strength and weakness. The goal of instruction is to adapt to and include this diversity no matter what its cause or its manifestations. The danger with a category such as learning disability is that the label can easily stigmatize [see Cushner, McClelland, and Safford (1992), for a discussion] and that it becomes too easy to avoid responsibility for adequate instruction. Moreover, the assumed purpose for labelling students as learning disabled is to develop a series of differential treatments for them that will facilitate their achievement. In our opinion, in many cases these treatments are all too often short-lived, uncoordinated, and ineffectual. Nevertheless, there are undoubtedly students for whom the label of learning disabled or ADHD is appropriate. Some of these students can benefit from medication. The problem for education, therefore, is to assure that students receive the type of special services that they need (which all too often means that the student must be classified) without the negative consequences so often contingent on this classification. Clearly, with the recent trend in this direction, most teachers will have students in their classroom who have been classified as learning disabled and/or ADHD and who may be on medication. At the very least, teachers need to be aware of the issues involved in this classification and need to have at their disposal a variety of techniques to deal with these students' special needs.

GIFTED AND TALENTED

Although it may seem unusual to discuss gifted students in the same section as the learning disabled, in fact many of the underlying issues are similar. As in our previous discussion, two of the major concerns are how the construct should be defined and how this form of diversity should be handled within the regular classroom. As before, both issues are controversial.

Definitions of Giftedness

While most general definitions of giftedness are fairly similar, considerable variability exists when the construct is made specific. The following quotation by Gage and Berliner (1991) is fairly representative of a general definition:

> . . . the category of gifted and talented students usually includes those demonstrating high performance in one or more of the following areas: general intellectual ability, specific academic aptitude, creative or productive thinking, leadership, or the visual and performing arts. (p. 216)

A similar definition is reported by Cramer (1991) who summarized the responses of twenty-nine experts in the field of gifted education:

> Giftedness is the potential for exceptional development of specific abilities as well as the demonstration of performance at the upper end of the talent continuum; it is not limited by age, gender, race, socioeconomic status, or ethnicity. (p. 88)

Finally, Renzulli (1986), one of the leaders in this field, offers what he terms a "three-ring" definition of giftedness: above-average ability, task commitment, and creativity. [For a review of various definitions and the way they are used in school districts throughout the country, see Hunsaker (1991).]

Although all three of the above definitions provide a general framework by which giftedness can be considered, there are obvious problems in their lack of specificity: How is "high performance" defined? What is "exceptional development?" At what point do we decide that a student is at the "upper end" of the talent continuum? Questions such as these may not be troubling when the discussion is at a theoretical level; they become critical, however, when the decision must be made about the classification and placement of a specific student.

The controversy over definition touches almost all aspects of programming for gifted and talented students. There is, for example, a basic question of whether this type of diversity should include only giftedness (which almost always means high aptitude, often defined as high IQ), only talented (which usually means some form of artistic or creative ability, however defined), or both. Where definitions focus on giftedness, a common process for classification is to impose some cutoff score based on an assessment of ability through a standardized test. Assume, for example, that a school district intends to employ an IQ test as the measure of ability and that the criterion for possible admission into the gifted program is an ability level no less than two standard deviations above the mean. If the IQ test used has a mean of 100 and a standard deviation of 15, this means that giftedness would be defined as having an IQ of 130 or more. Assumably, this would make the rule for classification clear. In practice, however, several complexities arise. For one thing, the standard error of measurement for most tests of this type is at least three points. A student who obtains a score of 129 would, therefore, have a reasonable case to argue that he or she should be eligible for the gifted program. In addition, the average IQ in any specific district may be more or less than 100, thereby producing a variable cutoff score across districts. Finally, different IQ tests have different means and standard deviations, and different versions of the same test can vary in these characteristics. What seems clear and easy to implement becomes, in practice, complex and controversial. Moreover, all of the complexity that arises in defining giftedness pales in comparison to the problem of defining talented, a construct whose definition has almost no consensus and whose operationalization is, at best, in its infancy.

Programming for the Gifted

Another major issue in this area concerns the type of program that should be implemented for gifted and talented students after these students have been classified. Getzels and Dillon (1973) list thirty types of programs that are currently in existence across the country, ranging from separate schools, separate classes within a regular school, pullout programs several times a week, Saturday classes, and so on. As one might expect, given our previous discussions, there is no real consensus about what type of program is best. There is some agreement among leaders in the field that special programs for gifted and talented students should not be integrated into the regular classroom and that instruction should not simply be more of the same thing that is presented to the regular students. As Renzulli and Reis (1991) point out, the reform movement in education has, to some extent, had the effect of decreasing attention to gifted programs because many of these reform movements have focused on improving the academic performance of lower achieving students. Given the increasing budgetary restraints in many school districts, gifted programs have often been eliminated in favor of programs focusing on the development of basic skills.

Implications for Education

Including a section on gifted and talented students is an important part of a chapter on diversity because this aspect of diversity represents one of the richest resources in any classroom. In many important ways, however, the area has produced a series of controversies that render some of the possible gains from gifted education difficult to attain. One of these issues touches on the discussion earlier in this chapter concerning racial and/or social-class bias in IQ tests. If one of the central components in the definition of giftedness is IQ and if the traditional IQ test is assumed to be biased against minority groups, it would necessarily follow that minority students would be underrepresented in gifted programs. This is especially critical if a strict IQ definition of giftedness (such as the 130 and above criterion previously mentioned) is used as the sole component for classification and placement. If, for example, the average IQ of African-American students is lower than the average IQ of white students, then a smaller percentage of African-Americans will be classified as gifted when compared to whites. When it can be shown, or when it is believed, that this difference is related to cultural factors inherent in the test, then the decision rule to place students in the gifted program will be racially biased.

In response to this problem, many school districts have attempted to implement programs for identifying gifted and talented students by the use of multiple criteria. These criteria include, in addition to an IQ measure, such variables as achievement, nominations (parent, teacher, peer, or self), and various ways of assessing creativity. Although in theory such programs should avoid the problems in the use of the IQ as the sole criterion, in practice this does not always happen. As Reis (1989) points out, "If the youngster has extremely high scores or recommendations on all or many of the other criteria, the multiple criteria are often ignored in favor of a single indicator, an individually administered IQ test'' (p. 403). The essential point to be made in this regard is that the use of an IQ measure, even in conjunction with other criteria, will exclude children of limited English proficiency, low income, and minority backgrounds. Although a radical departure from current practice, it follows that without a commitment to abandon the use of intelligence tests in the identification process, the problem of identifying minority children as gifted or talented will remain.

Adams (1990) not only presents data demonstrating the underrepresentation of minority children in gifted programs, but she also goes further in examining the core definition that our society has created for giftedness. As she points out, we have defined giftedness from the perspective of the white, middle-class culture. It should be expected, therefore, that minority students will not be recognized as gifted when such a definition is applied.

In perhaps one of the most thought-provoking articles in this area, Hoge (1988) reviews the major problems with the concept of giftedness. In addition to the problem with definition that we have already mentioned, he lists three other concerns: 1) there is almost always a discrepancy between the official or conceptual definition of the construct and the operational definition created by the measuring instruments; 2) there is seldom any relationship between the definition of giftedness and the nature of the programming for the students classified; and 3) there is a wide gap between the expectations that society has come to place on giftedness and the operational and conceptual definition of the construct that is presented by the test makers. Although he perceives some positive recent developments in this area, he cautions that at present the construct of giftedness has enough serious problems to question its use in education.

We share the basic idea of Renzulli and Reis (1991) in their discussion of a movement from ''being gifted'' to ''the development of gifted behaviors.'' We have reproduced part of their argument below:

> Many people have been led to believe that certain individuals have been endowed with a golden chromosome that makes him or her ''a gifted person.'' The further use of terms such as ''the truly gifted,'' ''the highly gifted,'' ''the moderately gifted,'' and ''the borderline gifted'' only serve to confound the issue because they invariably harken back to a conception of giftedness that equates the concept with test scores. This issue has led us to advocate a fundamental change in the ways the concept of giftedness should be viewed. . . . We believe that labeling students as ''gifted'' is counterproductive to the education efforts aimed at providing supplemen-

> tary educational experiences for certain students. We believe that our field should shift its emphasis from a traditional concept of "being gifted" to a concern about the development of gifted behaviors in those youngsters who have the highest potential for benefiting from special educational services. (p. 34)

The implication we draw from Renzulli and Reis' statement is that any static, test-driven definition of giftedness that serves primarily to label and sort one group of students for special placement is unacceptable. Just as there are several intelligences, so are there many ways to be gifted and many different pedagogical implications which can be derived from the varying strengths that students bring to school.

SUMMARY

Giftedness, like learning disability, presents a source of diversity in the classroom. Both of these concepts demonstrate the possibilities and the problems that we introduced in the beginning of this book: When is it advantageous for a teacher to conceptualize his or her classroom as consisting of a homogeneous group of students? When is it preferable to think of the class as composed of recognizable subgroups of students (e.g., the gifted or the learning disabled) who can be taught in a more or less similar fashion, and when is it better to think of the classroom as containing a group of students each of whom is unique? This is not an issue of choosing a correct or an incorrect position because each of these ways of conceptualizing diversity is defendable and each is necessary at different times and under different circumstances. Because we have no easy answer to these complex questions, we have tried throughout this section to caution against the overreliance on simple schemes for labelling and classifying students. In our opinion, these schemes often confuse more than they clarify and are seldom based on sound research that demonstrates that they produce higher levels of achievement or a more manageable classroom.

PART III

Topics and Issues in Diversity

IN THIS FINAL section of the book we will present a series of topics and issues that are relevant to diversity. We do not contend that these topics are exhaustive or that we are including complete presentations of any of the topics we have decided to discuss. Rather, our intent is to provide a series of representative issues that anyone concerned with diversity in education should consider.

In Chapter 6 we will discuss assessment and the implications of diversity for assessing student learning and achievement and for diagnosing student learning problems. As we have done for the first two parts of the book, we have decided to focus on this issue because it is representative and critical. Chapter 7 will include a series of rather disparate issues, including the use of autobiography in understanding others, knowledge bases in diversity, pedagogy, action research, postmodernism, and social reconstruction. It will be evident that we do not always have answers for the issues that are posed by these topics or that we can resolve to anyone's satisfaction the dilemmas that these issues present. Our intent is to provide a starting point for reflection and thought with a few representative research studies and with suggestions for further reading.

CHAPTER 6

Assessment and Diversity

INTRODUCTION

AS WE HAVE emphasized throughout this book, the explicit recognition of diversity has implications for many aspects of educational practice. One of the primary areas where this movement has had an impact is in the assessment of student learning. There is no question that testing has been, and continues to be, a central reality in American classrooms. As a nation, we test our students more often, and for more reasons, than any other country. Traditionally, the major component of this testing has consisted of the norm-referenced standardized test, usually in a multiple choice format [see Madaus (1994), for an excellent review of the history of testing in America]. As the nation's schools have become more diverse, and as the idea has become more widely accepted that a diverse student population requires varied pedagogy, the validity, usefulness, and fairness of traditional tests have been brought into question.

In this chapter we will present the arguments for and against standardized tests, especially in view of the increased call for accountability, which has characterized the most recent reform movement. We will then present a brief overview of alternative assessment, including short descriptions of several types of assessments that have been proposed as replacements for standardized tests. Finally, we will attempt to evaluate the arguments of the proponents and critics of alternative assessment concerning the ability of this type of assessment to provide more fair evaluations for groups of students who have been historically disadvantaged by our educational system.

EDUCATIONAL REFORM AND THE CALL FOR ACCOUNTABILITY

Educational reform in America has usually been driven by national goals embedded in one form or another of political ideology. The current wave of reforms is remarkably similar to those of the past, especially in the way politicians and columnists attribute many of the nation's problems to flaws in the nation's schools and teachers, with a resulting call for a complete overhaul of the educational system. All that has really changed is the focus of these concerns. In previous reform movements the underlying motivation for change was political and military dominance, whereas the current reform movement is conceptualized with a primary focus on the nation's competitive economic concerns. That is, where once we were concerned with meeting the challenge of Sputnik, we now are asked to prepare ourselves more adequately for the global marketplace. In both cases, it is assumed that our competitive disadvantage is due to problems in our schools, and various reforms are proposed to remediate these problems. Throughout, it is contended that the schools must be made more accountable and that standardized tests should be the primary source of this accountability.

It should be of no great surprise, therefore, that accountability has become a key component in the recent educational reform movement. Both *American 2000* and *Goals 2000,* the two most recent statements of a national agenda for education, contain the call for new and universally administered standardized tests in the core areas of mathematics, science, English, geography, and social studies. The highly touted international achievement standards, the merits of widely differing restructuring efforts, and the differential effects of various instructional strategies as well as individual differences in learning ability and achievement are expected to be assessed by these tests. This point is excellently made in a recent chapter by Garcia and Pearson (1994):

> Politicians and business leaders point to our lack of centralized educational system with clearly established standards and a national assessment system that evaluates the extent to which students measure up. In their eyes, standards and accompanying assessments would drive everything from classroom instruction to instructional materials to teacher education. Accordingly, the more that key educational milestones can be tied to the attainment of standards, the greater the likelihood that reform will move ahead. (p. 337)

Assumably, then, all the significant outcomes of education can be objectively measured, and the preferred method of such measurement is the standardized test. And because, implicitly or explicitly, assessment continues to drive the curriculum, the nature of this assessment has become one of the major issues of concern and controversy in contemporary educational practice.

Given the stream of controversy in which educational assessment is embedded, it is a formidable challenge to deal with issues of assessment in the context of this book in which differences associated with diversity are highly valued. As we have pointed out elsewhere (DuCette, Shapiro, and Sewell, 1992; Shapiro, DuCette, and Sewell, 1993), accountability and diversity almost inevitably lead in opposite directions. That is, the call for accountability and standardization leads to a unitary curriculum that can be assessed in approximately the same way at approximately the same time in all parts of the country. Diversity, on the other hand, leads to uniqueness in the curriculum, to the reflection of individual learning styles in assessment techniques, and to the minimization of direct comparisons between individuals. In an era of reform in which accountability is considered critical, diversity in all its aspects usually loses out to uniformity.

Despite this, it is important to document that the history of assessment, particularly in reference to standardized testing, is replete with legal and legislative decisions that have attempted to protect the constitutional rights of students from multiculturally diverse backgrounds (Samuda, 1975). These actions are especially pronounced in the efforts to provide equality of educational opportunities to students of color and/or students labelled and classified as individuals with disabilities. As we will note later in this chapter, these *de jure* safeguards are not always effective, and standardized tests have been viewed as limiting both access to and attainment in higher level education. This social and political argument is well captured by Darling-Hammond (1994):

> Though many proponents argued that the use of these tests as a tool for tracking students would enhance social justice, the rationales for tracking—like those for using scores to set immigrations quotas into the United States—were often frankly motivated by racial and ethnic politics. Just as Goddard's 1912 data "proving" that 83 percent of Jews, 80 percent of Hungarians, 79 percent of Italians and 87 percent of Russians were "feebleminded"—were used to justify low immigration quotas for those groups, so did Termin's test data "prove" that Indians, Mexicans and Negroes should be segregated into special classes. Presumptions like these reinforced racial segregation and differential learning opportunities. (p. 10)

Since assessment is so critical in the current educational reform movement, and since standardized tests play such a central role in this movement, it is important to understand how proponents of standardized tests have attempted to deal with diverse groups within the framework of psychometric theory. A summary of certain approaches to this issue is presented in the following section.

THE PSYCHOMETRIC APPROACH TO DIVERSITY

Standardized, norm-referenced tests have been the cornerstone of the testing industry, an industry that has played a significant role in shaping the history of American education. The highly sophisticated quantitative psychometric model on which the standardized test is based is proclaimed to be one of the most telling accomplishments of psychology and education. Nevertheless, this rich history is tarnished by the intensive criticism of a systematic and philosophically charged insensitivity to the poor and lower classes (Schiff and Lewontin, 1986) and to minorities and children with learning problems who have been disproportionately placed in segregated educational programs widely regarded as dead end and inferior [(Samuda, 1975; Sewell, 1979; *P. Larry* vs. *Wilson Riles* (1979)].

In response to this criticism, the proponents of standardized testing have moved aggressively in the direction of diversifying the types of assessment while staying within the essential psychometric framework. Although these proponents now give at least lip service to broadening assessment to include more than one form, there is still a tendency to characterize standardized tests as real assessment whereas alternative forms are considered watered down and auxiliary. For example, there is evidence in the literature on gifted education that when a variety of criteria are used to choose students for gifted education, among which is an IQ test, the IQ test will almost always carry most of the weight in the selection process. This example, which could be multiplied many times, demonstrates that the growing concern about standardized tests has not changed the fact that these tests still represent the "coin of the realm" (Haladyna, Nolen, and Haas, 1991) in the assessment of student achievement and ability. Moreover, it is clearly unfair to imply that the proponents of these tests are unaware of the issues or that they have not derived procedures that they believe meet the objections of the critics. While this issue is complex and sophisticated, one of the ways that the psychometric approach to diversity can be summarized is by the following three procedures [more exhaustive discussions can be found in Garcia and Pearson (1994) and in Kaplan and Saccuzzo (1989)]:

(*1*) The inclusion of diverse groups in the norming sample – One of the common criticisms of norm-referenced, standardized tests, especially those that were developed more than twenty years ago, is that these tests were normed and the test statistics were computed on samples which were exclusively or at least largely, composed of white, middle-class subjects. As such, critics of these tests have argued that the tests were biased against groups that were not represented in the norming sample. In response, the testing companies have tried in recent years to guarantee that the samples on which the test is normed approximate the population statistics of the larger American society.

(*2*) The explicit inclusion of diversity in the validity panel—One of the procedures that is now commonly used to validate any large-scale achievement or ability test is to convene a validity panel to evaluate the test as a whole and to rate each item on the test for bias. If correctly composed, these validity panels will include all relevant groups on whom the test will be used. Theoretically, therefore, this panel should be able to exclude items that are biased against any subgroup.

(*3*) The search for statistical bias at the full-scale or item level—In order to fully understand the complexity of this issue, a brief presentation of test bias as this is defined in the psychometric literature may help to clarify some of the confusion in this area. Assume that a test has been constructed with the purpose of making some type of yes-no decision (e.g., to hire someone, to admit someone to college, to certify someone for some role, to give some students "A's" and others "B's," etc.). As this is defined in the psychometric literature, this test is being constructed to make a prediction about future success, so the major issue is the test's predictive validity. Assume further that there is some explicitly defined criterion of success that can be expressed as a single decision point (a pass or "cut" score; a GPA which is minimal to graduate, etc.). Assume further that this test is given to a large number of subjects but that no decision is made on the basis of the test scores (i.e., everyone who takes the test is allowed to matriculate, everyone is hired, or whatever the context in which the test is being used). For demonstration purposes, assume that the test is being used to hire members of the police force. Everyone who applies is given the test, and everyone is hired. At the end of a year, each person who took the test is assessed and a decision is made as to whether the person has been successful or unsuccessful. As many books on standardized tests have pointed out, this situation produces a matrix with four quadrants as demonstrated in Figure 6.1.

As a psychometrician would look at this, all subjects in quadrants B and C represent correct decisions. That is, subjects in quadrant B were predicted to succeed and did so, whereas subjects in quadrant C were predicted not to succeed and they also fulfilled this prediction. Subjects in quadrants A and D represent mistakes or errors. Subjects in quadrant D were predicted to do well but, in fact, did not perform adequately. In test statistic jargon, these subjects are considered "false positives." Subjects in quadrant A, on the other hand, were predicted not to do well but, in fact, succeeded. These subjects are considered "false negatives."

Almost all of the issues on test bias are focused on quadrant A. Statistically, if the proportion of subjects from any specific subgroup (e.g., females or African-Americans) in quadrant A is exactly equal to their proportion in the population as a whole, then the test is considered statistically unbiased. If, on the other hand, any specific subgroup is underpredicted (i.e., the proportion of this group in quadrant A is higher than in the population as a whole), then the test is considered biased against that subgroup. Consider the case depicted in Figure 6.2 where M's represent males and F's represent females. Assume that half of the subjects who took the test are males and half females.

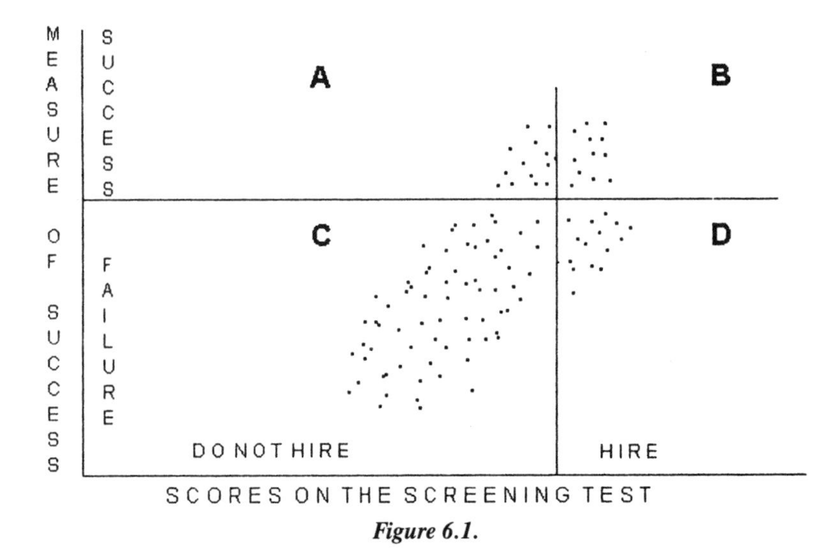

Figure 6.1.

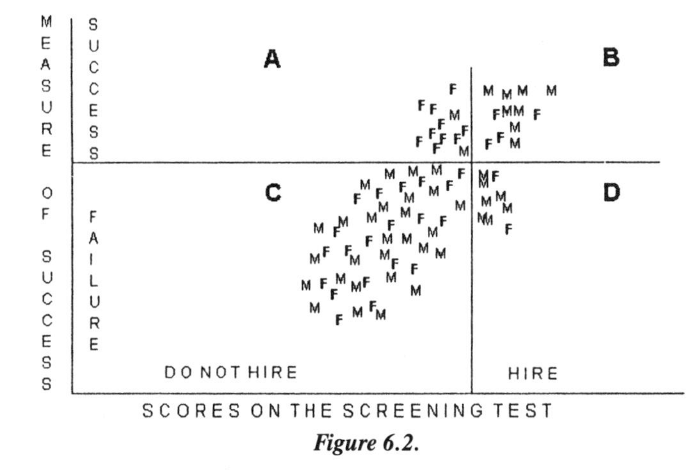

Figure 6.2.

It is evident that the test is biased against females because the proportion of females in quadrant A is higher than the proportion of males and therefore higher than their proportion in the entire sample.

Those who believe in standardized tests, and who are proponents of the psychometric tradition, believe that all tests can be made to be unbiased by a careful construction process in which all groups are adequately represented in the norming sample and in the validity panel. In addition, sophisticated statistical procedures have been developed to discover and eliminate individual items that are biased. Although this may push the psychometric argument a bit further than its own proponents would push it, it can be argued that, by the logic just presented, diversity should represent no special issue in test construction and use as long as careful safeguards are put in place.

THE CASE OF TEST UNFAIRNESS

As might be expected in an issue this controversial, the case is not as simple as was just presented. This has been pointed out by, among others, Cronbach (1975). Assume that a procedure identical to the one presented above was in place and that it produced the following data (Figure 6.3) (where, again, males are represented by M's and females are represented by F's).

The results show, as the term is defined psychometrically, that this test

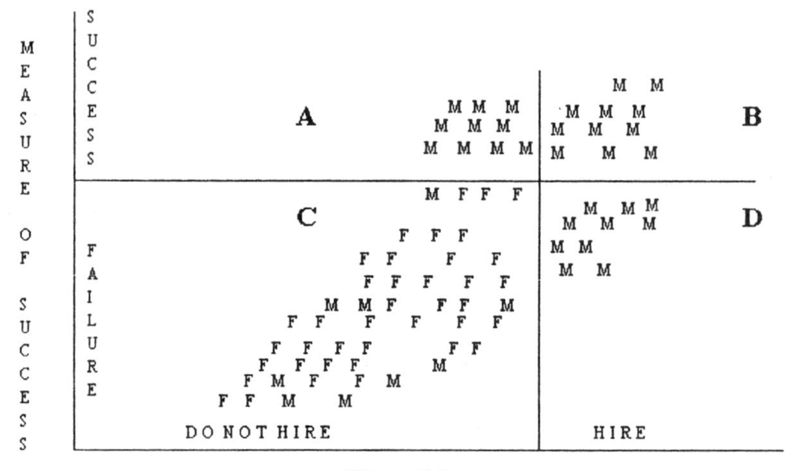

Figure 6.3.

is not biased because females have not been underpredicted. In fact, all females have been correctly predicted because the test predicts that all females will fail and this is exactly what has happened. As Cronbach has pointed out, this is a case where both success on the test and success on the criterion have been defined totally from a male perspective. For example, if the test is essentially a measure of physical strength, if success in policework is defined solely to reflect those aspects of the job that involve physical strength, and if women are generally less strong than men, then the test accurately reflects the criterion and it is making accurate predictions. Statistically, the test is not biased; it is, however, unfair.

To extend this argument into the educational literature, proponents of standardized tests, and specifically the IQ test, point out that the test is performing exactly as it was constructed to perform. That is, the test was designed to predict achievement in school and, within acceptable statistical limits, it does so with a fair degree of precision. Even if we forget for a moment that the test was designed to predict group performance, and that it cannot do as adequate a job in application to an individual, there is still the issue of test fairness. Because there are groups within this society who have been systematically excluded from those experiences and advantages that facilitate performance both on the test and on school achievement, it follows that the test will accurately demonstrate that one variable will correlate and predict another. But is this fair? Moreover, because standardized tests are arguably more open to bias and unfairness than are other types of assessments, limiting assessment to standardized tests almost guarantees that students who are less advantaged will be predicted to perform more poorly in the future.

This point is reinforced by Garcia and Pearson (1994) in their discussion of how some of the basic premises of psychometric theory work against diversity. As part of the regular validity process for a standardized test, the correlations of individual items against the total test score are usually computed. These item-to-total correlations are used to decide which test questions should remain on the final version of the test, with those demonstrating the lowest correlations usually being eliminated. As Garcia and Pearson point out, this procedure, which is an accepted part of test construction, guarantees that precisely those items on which the lowest scoring students did well will be eliminated. In their words, this mainstream bias in formal testing systematically works against members of groups that are not members of the dominant culture. It is this type of reasoning that causes many proponents of diversity in education to argue that assessment must go beyond standardized tests if equality of educational opportunity is to be achieved for all groups.

THE SOCIAL CONTEXT OF TESTING

If the issues in assessment were only philosophical arguments between academics, there would be little that would need our attention. The implications of testing, however, go far beyond theoretical speculations. Much of the controversy surrounding standardized tests has focused on cognitive assessment, particularly in reference to the use of IQ tests as a measure of intelligence. Despite these controversies, the psychometric approach, with its sophisticated quantitative methodology for providing comparative data, makes it an ideal vehicle to satisfy the public's demand for accountability in education. Standardized tests produce scores, and scores seem to provide the type of easily interpretable benchmark that educational reformers (as well as parents, school boards, and columnists) apparently need. The fact that these scores may be invalid reflections of a student's true ability or true achievement is often considered less important than the objectivity which these tests seem to provide. The equally troubling fact that these tests, at times, have deleterious effects on the curriculum, on the teachers who deliver this curriculum, and on the students who are the recipients of this curriculum is often also ignored. A central fact about the current social climate is that standardized tests meet a need (whether real or artificial) and do so better than any alternative that is currently available.

Again, if this were merely an academic issue, the problem would be troubling but not critical. The more basic issue is that these tests often lead to educational prescriptions that are incorrect and harmful. The emphasis on the psychometric approach, whether for the measurement of cognitive ability, academic achievement, or scholastic aptitude, has often led to differential treatment, which has too often constituted a denial of educational opportunity for some segments of our diverse population. It seems inevitable that standardized tests will be used to evaluate the effectiveness of educational reform initiatives. In fact, the proponents of these reforms clearly envision the improvement in standardized tests as the major (or, perhaps, sole) criterion to validate that their vision of higher standards has been achieved. We are concerned, however, about the tradition in testing that tends to compare the performance of students while ignoring glaring disparities in the opportunity to learn. Thus, significant differences in sociocultural experiences, inequities in school funding, and disparities in curriculum content and instructional resources are factors that are too often ignored when test results are used to compare students, teachers, schools, or school districts. In recent years, the normal response to this type of criticism is to cite the potential of alternative assessment to remediate the glaring problems in standardized tests. In fact, the notable shift from measurement and testing to assessment is perhaps coincidentally related to the current interest in many forms of alternative assessments.

If we accept the premise that accountability is necessary and assume that standardized tests will inevitably comprise one element of the assessment process, a broadened assessment process that includes a variety of measurement instruments becomes absolutely crucial. But by what criteria will we determine the choice of tests or procedures? From a psychometric perspective, whether the purpose of assessment is focused on cognitive, achievement or personality factors, the emphasis will be on tests and measurement approaches in which psychometric properties such as validity and reliability are well established. Others will unquestionably raise issues concerning the negative consequences or outcomes inherent in the psychometric tradition of testing. Thus, they are likely to propose nonstandardized alternative assessment approaches to meet a variety of assessment objectives without giving the technical psychometric criteria primary consideration.

Our intention to highlight differences among an increasingly diverse population with the objective of examining individual and group differences in learning and achievement suggests that no one model of assessment can fulfill the political, professional, and individual purposes of assessment. Differences in achievement attributable to factors related to learning styles, sociocultural experiences, race and ethnic distinctiveness, and levels of ability necessarily require an assessment system diverse in conceptualization, ideology, methodology, and purpose. In this context, we will focus briefly on several orientations to assessment. These approaches will diversify the assessment process to satisfy a wide range of purposes associated with accountability, learning, and instructional processes and diagnostic objectives.

ALTERNATIVE ASSESSMENT AND DIVERSITY

It follows from everything that has been said up to this point that the choice of assessment procedures should be dictated by the testing objectives. Darling-Hammond (1994) states this well in her summary of the lack of educational utility of many standardized tests.

> For most of this century, much of the energy of the U.S. measurement experts has been invested in developing tests aimed at ranking students for sorting and selecting them into and out of particular placements. Standardized test developers have devoted much less energy to worrying about the properties of these instruments as reflections of—or influences on—instruction. As a consequence, the tests generally do not reflect actual tasks educators and citizens expect students to be able to perform, nor do they stimulate forms of instruction that are closely connected to development of performance abilities.

Along with our belief that the testing objectives should determine the choice of assessment procedures, we also agree with Darling-Hammond's statement,

> We need some measures that would allow students to pursue their own strengths, interests, and ways of demonstrating knowledge. (Viadero, 1994, pp. 24–25)

Wiggins (1989, 1991, 1993) makes essentially the same point in calling for the creation of more authentic and equitable assessment techniques. He presents a powerful argument that educational assessment should use standards, but that standardization, in its common psychometric sense, should be eliminated. Wiggins is not alone in his thinking as there is a widely accepted rationale against standardized tests because of their inherent biases against poor and minority children. Their elimination has been frequently discussed, particularly when these tests are used to make high-stake decisions about students.

However, because of our belief that assessment choices should be appropriate to testing objectives, we are aware that as long as educational accountability is a goal, there will continue to be expectations that some kinds of standardized comparisons be made. Turning away from a psychometric approach to assessment, it seems to us that alternative assessment approaches have the potential to recognize students' instructional needs and their differences in learning styles, as well as the enormous shift in teaching/learning processes based on new standards and new knowledge bases in curriculum content. Despite the recent trend towards using these methods to attain the goal of accountability, underlying the alternative or authentic approaches is a continuing emphasis on the instructional process of learning, particularly from a longitudinal perspective.

The new forms tend to be more qualitative than quantitative. They also tend to be more process than product oriented, although they do include such approaches as performance assessment, which can be thought of as an end product, but preferably not in a standardized test format (Hutchings, 1989). Forms of performance assessment may include portfolios (i.e., Belanoff and Dickson, 1991; Camp, 1990; Hutchings, 1990; Murphy and Smith, 1990; Walters and Gardner, 1991; Walters and Seidel, 1991) student journals, dialogic journals and teacher logs (i.e., Cohen, Landa, and Tarule, 1990; Silberman, 1989) and other innovative assessment approaches designed to determine what students are learning over time. These types of assessment are open to multiple forms of assessment, including dynamic assessment (Fuerstein, 1979; Sewell, 1987). Above all, they resist labelling a student based on a single test result.

Complex times and complex knowledge bases require complex ways of assessing what students have learned. However, rather than try to cover all of the new forms of authentic assessment that are being introduced in this era, we will focus briefly on three of them. These three are quite different from one another and give some sense of the range and variety in the area of authentic or alternative assessment. Those we will turn to are: dynamic assessment, portfolio assessment, and performance assessment.

Dynamic assessment (Fuerstein, 1979; Sewell, 1987) is a process-sensitive model of assessment designed to facilitate the instructional needs of students. It is distinguished from traditional procedures by a distinct shift from a static to a dynamic orientation. By systematically engaging the student in structured tasks, dynamic assessment can do the following: 1) evaluate the individual' s problem-solving skills, 2) specify the conditions under which optimal learning can be achieved, 3) determine the level of intervention necessary to acquire new learning principles and transferrable skills, and 4) provide information on the effects of selective feedback and incentives on behavioral patterns. The direct assessment of cognitive processes from a structured learning experience minimizes the impact of several theoretical and practical issues associated with the assessment of ethnic minority students. Specifically, the direct involvement in a learning task to determine cognitive strengths and weaknesses or levels of academic functioning avoids the problem of making inferences about learning ability based on past learning experience or socioeconomic status.

Yet another promising alternative approach is *performance assessment* (Chittenden, 1991). Its focus on the direct measurement of performance has the distinct advantage of assessing complex processes associated with the learning or mastery of specific tasks across the curriculum in a variety of contexts. It is frequently viewed as a culminating project for students to accomplish as one final test of "knowledge in action" (Hutchings, 1989). This concept stemmed from the arts where a senior-level recital, exhibit, or performance of some kind occurred. Performance assessment has the potential to affect achievement through the motivation of students, their academic assessment and self-assessment, and the monitoring of their personal growth.

Portfolio assessment has been defined by Hutchings (1990) as one form of performance assessment which involves the collection of student work done over time. It has also been defined by Walters and Seidel (1991) as "a record of learning that focuses on students' work and their reflections on that work" (p. 1). Beyond these broad definitions, the collection or record is often varied – some portfolios include only written work, others contain a broader array of materials that may resemble products (Hutchings, 1990).

Perhaps portfolio assessment has emerged as a major form of alternative assessment because of the variety of decisions related to instruction that the portfolio can be used to make. From an instructional perspective, Murphy and Smith (1990) cited essential features of the teaching/learning process –

motivating students, self-assessment, monitoring personal growth, curriculum revisions—in which portfolio assessment can be used.

Unquestionably, the most positive aspect of portfolio assessment is its focus on self-assessment for the student (Walters, Seidel, and Gardner, 1994). Critical appraisal of one's own work should ultimately lead to higher-level thinking in addition to providing rich products for assessment (Tittle, 1991). For example, in asking students to choose their best and worst work, and then by asking them to reflect on the reasons why they have made their choices, teachers can learn a great deal about the cognitive processes of their students. Above all, students can learn a great deal about themselves and reflect upon how and what they learn.

Although many of the critical issues in alternative assessment, such as the need for conceptual clarity and a mechanism for self-criticism, are yet to be fully resolved (Worthen, 1991), the opposition to the traditional use of standardized, norm-referenced tests has been the impetus for well-informed educators to contribute meaningful language, methodology, and political ideology to the assessment debate.

Arguing from a feminist perspective in the realm of alternative assessment, Shapiro (1992) advanced several guiding principles for an assessment approach sensitive to diversity issues. Out of the need to meet conflicting demands of accountability and diversity in the interdisciplinary area of women's studies came a new form of assessment—feminist assessment. Not surprisingly, a fundamental principle in this form of assessment, as described in the project entitled, *The Courage to Question* (McTighe, 1992), was the necessity for all assessment related decisions to be questioned in a context that is student centered. Additionally, this form of assessment questions almost everything related to assessment, is participatory, is affected by its context or institutional culture, and is also affected by its content and methodology. Feminist assessment provides a broad framework in which issues can be discussed. Above all, it assumes questioning is expected regarding all forms of assessment and evaluation and their ultimate uses.

Arguing from the point of view of the critical theorist regarding an alternative to traditional assessment is the emancipatory theory of Giroux (1992b) and others. Giroux advocates a public language that in many ways could replace the language of assessment. According to Giroux, "This language would refuse to reconcile schooling with forms of tracking, testing, and accountability that promote inequality by unconsciously ignoring cultural attributes of disadvantaged racial and class minorities" (p. 8). Giroux develops open-ended, thoughtful questions that have implications for both the curriculum and for outcomes-based assessment. He asks: What kinds of citizens do we hope to produce through public education? What kind of society do we want to create?

Giroux's public language moves us away from a product model of assessment. He leads us towards a process of growth and a language of critique and possibilities. His judgement of what students learn focuses on what kind of citizens they will become. Ultimately, students would be expected to emerge as "critical citizens who are capable of exercising civic courage and the moral leadership necessary to promote and advance the language of democracy" (Giroux, 1992b, p. 8). Such comprehensive long-term outcomes are hard to assess. However, we would know that the goals had been achieved by the changes noted in our society. These changes would be demonstrated primarily through a grass-roots youth movement towards equality and social justice.

SUMMARY

Assessment is at the heart of the educational process. Test-generated data are powerful tools influencing an individual's future, instructional quality, and political decisions. Clear choices must be made related to the selection of the assessment approach or approaches for the intended purposes. It should be obvious by now, from the presentation in this section, that our own choice would lead us away from the "tried and true" path of standardized tests. Combining these tests with alternative forms of assessment is less objectionable. However, if the perceived crisis in American education is generated from the sense that the academic performance of American students is deficient, the continued use of traditional testing practices will simply further document what we already know rather than promote and enhance achievement.

A fundamental goal of the current reform movement in education is to improve the quality of students' academic performance. Assessment and testing should contribute to teachers' instructional strategies, which are the *sine qua non* of the requirements associated with achievement. Assessment conceptualized as a vehicle to enhance achievement rather than for providing data for comparative analysis has the potential, via alternative assessment models, to deal effectively with the content, pedagogy, and student population related to diversity.

Quality instruction implies an understanding of what to teach, how to transmit knowledge, and a sound grasp of what students know. Thus, the goals of accountability are partially factored into the approaches associated with alternative assessment. But more importantly, alternative assessment has the potential to assess students' learning and knowledge even when the curriculum is richly enhanced by materials that reflect cultural compatibility with the issues of race, social class, gender, and other categories of difference. In contrast, standardized measures are unlikely to generate information on students' problem-solving skills, a meaningful understanding of their strengths and weaknesses, and the optimal conditions under which learning occurs. Gathering data on what students know through the static objective measures of standardized tests will neither be enlightening nor valuable for the teaching/learning process.

Throughout this section, we have spoken of authentic or alternative assessment outside the standardized format. It is clear, however, that this way of looking at alternative assessment is changing. Already, work is progressing towards test preparation to meet national standards focusing on the use of "the 3P's"—performance, portfolios, and products" (Madaus, 1993, p. 10). Within the psychometric model there are ongoing attempts to design standardized tests that will incorporate the well-established technical qualities of validity, reliability, and other technical features while delivering alternative assessment practices. For example, Sternberg (1990) and Gardner and Hatch (1989) are developing assessment instruments focusing on multiple intelligence that will likely capture a wider range of abilities in diverse populations (see the presentation in Chapter 5 for a discussion of this issue).

Although there are some outstanding psychometricians and psychologists working in the area of standardizing authentic assessment, there are some real drawbacks in using this type of assessment in high-stake testing and as a policy tool of the government (Darling-Hammond, 1991; Jaeger, 1991; McLauglin, 1991; Shepard, 1991; Stake, 1991). The misuse of authentic assessment has the potential to once again keep those who are different in their place; it has the potential to sort, track, and sift those who are different from the norm. Nevertheless, we believe that authentic assessment, used by teachers in the classroom to diagnose and improve instruction, has the potential to be a very important and powerful tool. We also believe that authentic assessment, in the hands of the student, can be an equally powerful tool for self-reflection and growth.

Through alternative assessment models, as we define them, the way is open for educators to begin to ask appropriate questions as well as have the courage to ask the hard questions related to accountability, the improvement of instruction, and diversity. Such questions might include: Can educators continue to use standardized test performance results as the major determinant of a student's success? Do such results really demonstrate what a student has learned over time? What is the link between content, pedagogy, and assessment? How should one assess student learning of issues of diversity? Who should determine the approach or approaches regarding assessment used in American schools–educators, legislators, taxpayers, psychometricians? Should we react to the attempts to standardize authentic assessment? What part should standardization play when working with diverse populations? And whose standards are we privileging anyway?

CHAPTER 7

Other Topics and Aspects in Diversity

AUTOBIOGRAPHY AND DIVERSITY

> Autobiography can become an act of telling and listening to each other's stories, an exercise in understanding and extending our own social history. The telling of life stories gives us clues to the present as well as hints of the future. It provides the possibility of becoming more conscious, more intentional. (Ayers, 1992, p. 48)

IN THE PROLOGUE of this book, we provided you with brief autobiographies. In our stories, we emphasized pivotal aspects of our backgrounds as well as critical incidences that showed our awakening to areas of diversity. Although our stories offered some disclosures, they were primarily focused stories intent on making some points related to diversity. For us, these narratives are ongoing, for in our dual roles as joint authors and as members of the leadership team of our college, we continue our dialogue to learn more about each other as well as to learn more about our different ways of looking at the world. The sharing of our narratives has not only helped us to trust each other but also it has given us new respect of different aspects of diversity and has enabled each of us to walk in each others' shoes. In particular, in our role as administrators, such understanding of others is needed when we seek to understand those we are asked to assist and work with, such as faculty, students, the university community and the local community—to name but a few of the constituencies that have impact on our working lives.

A goal throughout this book has been to broaden the dialogue to include not only teachers but also educational administrators in studying, understanding, and appreciating diversity. Unlike much of the recent educational autobiographical work that focuses primarily on teachers, we feel it is important to move beyond the classroom walls and include the school administrator in the process. There is a need for administrators of schools as well as administrators in higher education to find out who they are and where they derived their beliefs regarding other groups within society. We feel that these times for self-reflection can make a difference as to how they lead and work with others. In fact, from our own personal experiences in sharing, we know that this is true.

There are many studies, for example, that focus on the importance of the principal as instructional leader (Bolman and Deal, 1991; Hetrick, 1990; Lightfoot, 1983; Mitchell, 1990). The principal's vision can move a school along in a certain direction. If this is the case, then surely such leaders need to be immersed in the process of learning and caring about diversity. In speaking with administrators regarding reflection and study, they frequently say that they simply do not have the time for such endeavors. However, we believe that they must make the time, because diversity, as a concept, cannot be ignored as a critical influence in American education. In an era when the demographics are shifting, it is essential that educational administrators make the time to self-reflect, learn about others, and, in so doing, hopefully understand and empathize. Through this process, they can have a profound effect on shaping the vision of not only their school but also of its community as well.

Grumet (1978) indicates the importance of self-reflection to enable us to pull away and view an emotional incident with more objectivity. She says that "autobiography, like teaching, combines two perspectives, one that is a distanced view—rational, reflective, analytic, and one that is close to its subject matter—immediate, filled with energy and intention" (p. 212).

Such distancing can make a difference to educators who teach and lead and have to make important decisions that have impact on others. Pulling back enables us to review our own emotions to determine why we are finding certain decisions so difficult. These moments of self-reflection, developed by writing or telling our own stories, are bound to make a difference in how we lead or teach. Additionally, being able to pull back and ask ourselves how someone of a different gender, social class, or culture might feel when this decision is made can lead to more wise and inclusive decisions. In the area of diversity, for example, important questions that a good leader needs to ask in making any decision are: Who have I omitted? How can I frame this decision to make it more inclusive?

Teachers and Autobiography

Throughout this book, we highlighted a salient issue that few books on diversity and education discuss in any depth. This issue deals with the demographic mismatch of a homogeneous teaching profession composed of predominately white, upwardly mobile, working-class women, and at the same time, the growing diversity of the student body. This striking discontinuity could be viewed in a negative light or, alternatively, it may be framed in a more positive manner. Although we choose the latter, we do feel that this discontinuity should be discussed. To deal with some aspects of the perceived mismatch, we believe that autobiography can be a powerful approach to assist female teachers to come to terms with who they are, what their current beliefs are concerning diversity, where those beliefs come from, and how they have chosen and will choose to deal with differences in the future.

Through the use of autobiography, we do not ignore the backgrounds that new teachers bring to the university classroom. Hutchinson and Johnson (1993–1994) explained this well, when they wrote:

> Prospective teachers do not enter teacher training programs "tabula rasa," ready to be imprinted with the knowledge and skills of teaching. Instead, they come with many perspectives about the teacher role which they have formulated with the influence of significant others (parents, teachers, friends) and events (home, school, community). Prospective teachers begin to develop these perspectives about teaching long before entering colleges and universities. (p. 61)

Kennedy (1992) reiterated Hutchinson's and Johnson's point by indicating that "research continues to find that teachers learn a great deal about teaching from their own experiences" (p. 65).

There is rich literature in the area of women's studies and, in particular, those studies about women in education that can assist teachers in the self-reflection process. For example, works by writers such as, Gilligan (1982), Gilligan, Ward, and Taylor (1988), Noddings (1984, 1991, 1992), and Belenky et al. (1986), to name but a few, have opened the way to an appreciation of women's ways of knowing and of educating others. Although the current literature in the area of women's autobiography, narrative, and self-reflection is burgeoning, it is also important to remember that this kind of work has a long history. Initially through feminist presses and journals and later on in mainstream publications, a vast array of women's diaries, letters, journals, memoirs, and autobiographies written from the 19th century to the present have provided important information for women about their foremothers at home and at work (Howe, 1984). In particular, there are diaries and writings of teachers and of other educators that can serve to inform us [i.e., Chamberlin (1981); Hoffman (1988)].

However, we believe that there is nothing as helpful as studying our own lives to help determine who we are and where we are going. In fact, it is reassuring to note that there seems to be a trend in many of the current courses in teacher education and in educational administration to include journal writing as part of the assignments. Journal writing can be an effective vehicle to assist the new teacher in finding her authentic voice. It may prove to be extremely important in helping her to take on the role of a professional and in preparing to position herself as a leader. Finding ones authentic voice can mean a great deal and can enable many a young woman, who has often been silenced, to speak. Lorde (1984), Heilbrun (1988), Shapiro and Smith-Rosenberg (1989), and many others have noted the strength of journal writing and what a powerful means it can be to combat oppression and repression. Cooper (1991) expresses this well when she stated,

> Writing in a journal is thus a way to attend to the self, to care for and to feed oneself. It can be a place to dump anger, guilt, or fear instead of dumping it on those we love. It can be a place to clarify what it is we feel angry or guilty about. It can be a place to encourage ourselves, to support ourselves, in working through that anger or guilt, and it can be a place to transform silence into language and action. (p. 105)

Voice need not always be discovered through writing. Much can be gleaned through oral histories and through conversations or dialogues. The study of oral histories can provide a sense of roots, while dialogues can challenge us to move beyond where we currently are in our acceptance and appreciation of our own backgrounds and hopefully of others. In many teacher education classes, there is a feeling of a single-sex classroom. Such a classroom can enable future female teachers to read some of the scholarship by and about women and feel safe to discuss the hard topics of self and others. We are certain that not enough teacher educators spend the time to provide those golden opportunities, focusing on gender issues, that may lead to connected knowing (Belenky et al., 1986). Those special discussion times, when ways of knowing connect with women's lives, can lead to important understanding. Additionally, those are also the special times when not only similarities but differences can be discussed in women's lives. It is a time to deal with issues of race/ethnicity, social class, disability, and other areas of difference that help to determine the world views of the future teacher. It is also the time to deal with the role of the male in society to try to better understand how both sexes' lives are socially constructed and the effect of the social construction of gender on the education of children.

School Administrators and Autobiography

Although the predominately female teaching force needs to be self-reflective, so too do the school administrators, the majority of whom continue to be white, middle-class males. This group requires time to find out about themselves in order to understand and deal with others. Masculinity in our society is frought with its own problems. The expectation of men as breadwinners carries a legacy that school administrators need to explore. One way to do this is through the autobiographies of educators and other role models. Just sharing another male's life experiences, even vicariously, can have a profound effect.

Beyond the readings, writing of ones' own experiences in a journal can make a difference. That ability to pull back and reflect can make decision making far easier and less stressful. If those reflections can be shared with others, in an educational leadership classroom, for example, much can be learned as assistance from others in similar situations can be shared. However, it is important that such discussions lead to questions and challenges. Along with the social construction of the male in our society, there needs to be exploration of male privilege in our culture. As the discussion of the male is explored, so should issues of race/ethnicity, social class, and other forms of differences be considered and debated. The multiple layering and/or the intersections of differences can have a powerful effect on how a male leader is perceived in our culture.

Different Forms of Autobiography

Autobiographies come in different forms and in many instances can help us tear down barriers of perceived differences. They also can be tailored to the needs of individuals who have different learning styles. For example, visual learners may gain a great deal from the movie focusing on the life's work of Jaimie Escalante, who taught underachieving Latino children mathematics and helped them to learn. It may serve to make connections when the work is focused on a particular group's life experiences, such as in Braxton's (1989) work where the focus is on black women writing their autobiographies. Some learners have naturally turned to, and enjoy keeping, autobiographies in the form of diaries and journals.

Autobiographies may be perceived as collaborative efforts rather than individualistic endeavors. It may be that the development of autobiographies in the form of case studies, such as those emanating from the Teacher Lore Project (Schubert, 1992), encourages teachers to share their stories and problems with others. They may appear as part of a series as in the case of the personal essays of thirty-three outstanding educators (Burleson, 1991). Autobiographies may appear in the form of dialogue, which is currently being encouraged as an ongoing way to provide people with a voice enabling them to discuss themselves, their problems, and their lives with others who care. Noddings has expanded this form of narrative in her concept of "interpersonal reasoning" (Noddings, 1991, p. 157). In interpersonal reasoning, Noddings believes that there are certain features that enable people to share their lives and fears with others and may lead to some related action. She speaks of the important features of an attitude of solicitude or care, attention, flexibility, effort aimed at cultivating relation, and a search for an appropriate response (p. 163).

Whether written, oral, alone, or in groups, the sharing of one's life, under safe and trusting conditions, can be a meaningful endeavor. We believe that this process can be important for both teachers and administrators and can provide a baseline enabling educators to move on to an understanding of themselves as well as the strangers among us.

Others or the Strangers among Us

The study and understanding of self, it is hoped, can enable educators to be ready to turn to others or the strangers among us.

Sabatay (1991) described a stranger in this way:

> The experience of being a stranger is a primary concern of many educators, writers, and social scientists. We all experience being strangers at different times, and we become aware that strangerhood has many nuances. We can be strangers by being in a new land; we can be strangers by virtues of any difference: physical, psychological, social, cultural, religious, political, racial, personal. One can be a stranger by remaining within oneself or by being at odds with the world. (p. 136)

Sabatay and other educators recommend once again the rubric of autobiography and storytelling for breaking down the barriers between oneself and others. They also recommend the importance of discussing when we have been strangers ourselves, such as in our visits to other cultures or in even attending a gathering in which we know no one and feel uncomfortable. Such recollections will serve to break down the barriers of difference and enable us not to be fearful but to be curious and interested in others. Lacking trust and loyalty, there is a need to secure something tangible from the stranger. And yet, as educators, isn't it better that we shared and learned rather than ignored them?

As educators, we continue to need to know about ourselves and others. By understanding our own backgrounds (the critical incidences that shaped our lives, and the time when consciousness- raising occurred as we dealt with difference) we believe that educators can better face the schools and classrooms in the 21st century. A focus on autobiography, we believe, is an important trend that has developed in education. Ayers (1992) indicated its impact well when he wrote,

> The modern interest in autobiography may be linked to the accelerating social, geographic, and political mobility characterizing society. In a world of constant change, of danger, confusion, and fear, autobiography can become an explanation and justification of who one has become. Autobiography can be a response to the flux, motion, chaos and noise of the environment, something Berger (1963) calls a "global historical phenomenon" and "a real existential problem in the life of the individual" (p. 65). Autobiography is an attempt to ground oneself and explain oneself in the whirlwind. (p. 45)

Ethics and Autobiography

While finding out about ourselves and how we perceive the strangers among us, ethics as an area cannot be ignored. Our own ethical values are bound to emerge as we journey through our own lives because often we have been placed in situations where ethical decisions have had to be made. It seems to us important that we, as educators, grapple with the processes we have used to make those decisions as well as the underlying philosophies that have guided us.

For example, it would do well to determine if our decisions are made from moral absolutist principles or from situational ethical perspectives. Additionally, a study of both traditional and nontraditional ethics relating to education can be very instructive. Knowledge of the writings of liberal democratic ethicists (i.e., Beauchamp and Childress, 1984; Dewey, 1902, 1938, 1957; Kohlberg, 1981, 1984; Starratt, 1994; Strike, Haller, and Soltis, 1988) compared with the critical theory ethicists (i.e., Foster, 1986; Freire, 1970; Freire and Shor, 1987; Greene, 1988, 1993; Greenfield, 1993; Purpel, 1989) compared with feminist ethicists (i.e., Beck, 1994; Belenky et al., 1986; Gilligan, 1982, 1988; Noddings, 1984, 1992; Shapiro and Smith-Rosenberg, 1989) as well as with ones who intersect with different groups (Stefkovich and Shapiro, 1995) can be exceedingly important from both personal and professional standpoints. Such critique and analysis can assist us in noticing the patterns that we tend to repeat in making decisions throughout our lives. As what was previously carried out at a more subconscious level now becomes visible through reflection, each of us has the opportunity to decide if these are the ways we want to continue to make decisions and if our decisions seem to us to be wise ones.

By understanding our ethical selves, we will be better prepared to understand our students and make the leap to understanding others or the strangers among us.

KNOWLEDGE BASES AND DIVERSITY

If one follows the process described in this book, each of us would then move, although not necessarily in a lock step pattern, from autobiography to categories of diversity from different knowledge bases depending upon our backgrounds and interests. In actual fact, that seems to be the way many of us now involved in diversity have moved into this broad interdisciplinary area. In our own case, we can provide examples of this as one of us comes to diversity having had considerable background in the area of women's studies; another has turned to the area through an extensive study of race and social class with a special emphasis on the problems those who are different face in taking IQ tests; and the other, with many years of training in the psychometric tradition, has made the leap and crossed the paradigms in an effort to learn more about the whole area of diversity rather than continue to read about this area remaining within the limits of a single discipline.

In this book, we have attempted to introduce the reader to some of the different knowledge bases one needs to know to begin to understand the complex area of diversity. The umbrella of diversity is wide, and it is important to read across the areas as well as read intensively in one or two categories. King (1994) stated our intentions in this book well when she wrote,

> A teacher's own self-awareness regarding matters of culture, ethnicity, educational purpose and societal injustice are all part of the sociocultural context knowledge that should be included in the knowledge base of teaching. (p. 42)

As we have begun to move across the categories of diversity, it becomes exceedingly difficult to determine which knowledge bases about the sociocultural context of education we should study. Besides finding it difficult to determine whose culture should be studied and respected, it is also hard to know whose voices to privilege and where the diverse cultures should fit into the curricula of the schools. There is always the danger of providing a great deal of information that might be deemed to be worthless in terms of what will be tested by powerful outside agencies (e.g., The Educational Testing Service or The Psychological Corporation). Issues that need to be addressed are: 1) Can we and/or should we place the knowledge bases of those who are different in the center of the curriculum? 2) If we do this, as we have done in the past with the Eurocentric curriculum, will we then repeat our mistakes and privilege one kind of experience and knowledge base over another? 3) Despite the worry of privileging some rather than all, there is a need to do something and do it soon so that African-American, Latino, and other students of color do not continue to drop out of high school at their current high rate.

What is clear is that students need to have some kinds of connected knowing experiences for learning to take place (Belenky et al., 1986). Hence, an Afrocentric curriculum may have a powerful effect on some students who find that the writings within the area of African-American Studies touch a cord and trigger experiences leading to understanding and cultural empowerment (Capper, 1993). Without a discussion of meaningful life experiences, alienation can occur (Felice, 1981; King, 1991; Steele, 1992; Trueba, 1988). Bowers and Flinders (1990) pointed out that teachers' professional knowledge has tended to be silent on the importance of understanding cultural patterns that have an effect on both teachers and students (King, 1991, p. 14).

Like King (1994) and Giroux (1992a), we have tried to broaden the professional knowledge base for teacher preparation. We have also attempted to go beyond education that conforms only to the interests and "imperatives of the market place." Additionally, we have attempted to indicate the importance of making the knowledge bases meaningful for those involved in the educational process.

Currently, there appear to be large gaps in the knowledge bases of teacher and administrative educators. In this book, we have attempted to provide discussions that emphasize differences rather than ask students to blend in to the current dominant Eurocentric curriculum. As educators, we are all a part of a deficit-oriented knowledge base. (We are aware of the pejorative nature of the deficit concept currently in the literature; however, in this case, we believe that all groups have deficits or limitations in their education in the area of diversity.) To make up for our deficiencies, much needs to be borrowed from areas such as women's studies, African-American studies, ethnic studies, and other interdisciplinary programs that focus on differences.

Although we believe that educators should make up their deficits by studying different categories of difference, we do not go as far as Welch in her determination to highlight differences but not seek commonalities. She expressed her belief this way,

> The aims of equality and respect are met by highlighting differences, not by transcending them or looking beneath them for a common foundation. (Welch, 1991, p. 83)

Unlike Welch, we tend also to seek that common bond, if at all possible, that will enable us to work together as a community. In this, we are more closely allied to Tim Westerberg, an outstanding principal from Littleton High School in Littleton, Colorado, who expresses his dilemma in the following manner:

> My biggest challenge has been to help a fairly diverse group in a pluralistic society to find a shared vision and still protect the diversity. (Steinhauer, 1994, p. 36)

Throughout this book, we have suggested that you, the reader, pick and choose among the areas of difference those categories that are connected to your life and work, as well as to the lives and work of those you are teaching or leading. We have tried to provide an introductory knowledge base under each of the categories in this book, enabling teacher and administrative educators to begin to rethink and even redesign their curricula and schools. We especially hope that the bibliography included in this book will help you embark on an exploration process into one or more category of difference.

PEDAGOGY AND DIVERSITY

> . . . pedagogy is always related to power. (Giroux, 1992c, p. 21)

In its most restrictive and literal definition, pedagogy refers to the teaching of children. When viewed from this narrow perspective, the knowledge bases on pedagogy and on instruction are highly similar and, in fact, largely overlap (Gore, 1993). Moreover, this focus on children leads to an almost exclusive interest on school-based learning and on the investigation of those principles which can be used to facilitate learning by children in school. Even broadening the concept of pedagogy by including the teaching of adults (which some have termed "andragogy" to distiguish this form of teaching from the traditional teaching of children) can at times merely mean that principles proven effective in the arena of traditional schools are used unquestionably in the nontraditional arenas in which adults learn. This way of thinking about pedagogy produces a focus on skills or practices which constitute the "craft" of teaching. It is the traditional way of defining pedagogy and it has been the basic undergirding of teacher and administrator preparation programs for many years. For us, and for the writers we will cite in this section of the chapter, the usefulness of this narrow definition is limited.

There is a broader way of thinking about pedagogy, as reflected in the *Ninth Edition of Webster's Dictionary. Webster's* defines pedagogy as an art, a science or a profession of teaching. This definition is a clear improvement over the narrow focus on teaching children, as it reflects the fact that teaching is a profession with its own set of issues, knowledge bases, ethics and skills. In fact, the definition is broad enough to enable educators, such as Goodlad (1990), to place this concept as central in his design for a school or center of pedagogy in each university or college that prepares teachers. As innovative as Goodlad's design is, however, the definition he has chosen still produces a discussion of pedagogy that focuses somewhat narrowly on skill acquisition. In fact, Goodlad uses the example of the relationship between teaching hospitals and the medical profession as a model of his pedagogical centers. While there is much to recommend this analogy, there are also cautionary notes to be sounded. In particular, the medical profession should not serve as the standard against which other professions are judged, and the type of skill focus which characterizes medical education is not an adequate model for teaching in its broadest sense.

Our preferred definition of pedagogy is broader than either of the definitions cited above. We choose this broad definition because we want those who are teachers and school administrators to understand, review, reflect upon, and analyze the full range of pedagogies. We also want educators to realize that the kind of pedagogy they practice impacts on society and, in return, society impacts on pedagogy. We are conscious that there is a wide range of pedagogies from which we can choose, whether it be traditional, critical, or feminist.

Thus, we share Giroux's (1991) definition of pedagogy, when he wrote,

> Pedagogy, in this case, is not defined as simply something that goes on in schools. On the contrary, it is posited as central to any political practice that takes up the question of how individuals learn, how knowledge is produced, and how subject positions are constructed. In this context, pedagogical practice refers to forms of cultural production that are inextricably historical and political. Pedagogy is, in part, a technology of power, language, and practice that produces and legitimates forms of moral and political regulation which construct and offer human beings particular views of themselves and the world. (p. 56)

Giroux's and our form of pedagogy can be practiced not only by teachers in a classroom but also by school administrators in their work with their faculty and students and by university faculty in their interactions with their students. The scope of pedagogy enables parents and community people to be included in thinking through how individuals learn, how knowledge is procured and how subject positions are constructed. It frames the debate widely and tends to be inclusive.

Along with Giroux's political and cultural foci, we also recognize the organizations and ordering of information and subjects related to pedagogy. Popkewitz's (1992) definition of pedagogy speaks to us as well when he stated,

> Pedagogy is not only a system of information or subjects that are organized for students but an ordering of social fields. The organization of school knowledge defines the categories and distinctions that legitimate what is to be thought about and interpreted in social affairs. In this deeper sense, pedagogy is a system of discipline by which hierarchies—markers of social distinction and aspirations—are established. (Weiler and Mitchell, 1992, p. 136)

Those "hierarchies—markers of social distinction," indicate that pedagogy is far from neutral. This lack of neutrality brings questions to mind—Who defines school knowledge? Who organizes school knowledge?—because ordering does occur and because many choices are made on behalf of others.

Ordering and politics seem to us to be primary concerns when one has to deal with diversity and/or multiculturalism. Popkewitz expressed this well when he stated,

> The rules of constructing pedagogy about multiculturalism also contain contradictions. It can decontextualize the culture of the "other" and reformulate experiences to respond to particular forms that hide moral, political, and social imperatives of schooling. In defining curriculum as

> a psychological problem, sets of values and social regulations are formulated. The dynamic sets of elements that underlie the social construction of culture are decontextualized and made into seemingly universal characterization. Where different cultures do make distinctions about the organization of time and space, the organization of curriculum discourse redefines and reformulates all experiences into universals, logical, and seemingly disinterested categories. (p. 146)

Our definition of pedagogy involves voices from the field of critical pedagogy (i.e., Giroux, Popkewitz) as well as many who are in the area of feminist pedagogy. Feminist pedagogy has been explained by Shrewsbury (1987) this way:

> Feminist pedagogy begins with a vision of what education might be like but frequently is not. This is a vision of the classroom as a liberatory environment in which we, teacher-student and student-teacher, act as subjects, not objects. Feminist pedagogy is engaged teaching/learning—engaged with self in a continuing reflective process; engaged actively with the material being studied; engaged with others in a struggle to get beyond our sexism and racism and classism and homophobia and other destructive hatreds and to work together to enhance our knowledge; engaged with the community, with traditional organizations, and with movements for social change. (p. 6)

Many feminists have contributed to the field known as feminist pedagogy, such as Brown and Hoffman (1991), Culley and Portugues (1985), Ellsworth (1989), Gabriel and Smithson (1990), Gore (1993), Lather (1991), Schniedewind and Maher (1987), Shapiro (1990), and Shapiro and Smith-Rosenberg (1989). It is a burgeoning field because feminists have a respect for pedagogy as well as a healthy fear of it. Henry (1993–1994) expressed this well when she wrote,

> The classroom is not a safe place. Teaching and learning about race/ethnicity, culture, religion, language background, socio-economic background, gender, sexuality, and able-bodiedness are difficult. Learning about these issues by examining our own lives, by tracing and exposing our personal and social histories is dangerous. (p. 2)

Those who turn to feminist pedagogy as well as critical pedagogy often refer to transformative pedagogy. Hooks (1993) described this when she wrote:

> Making the classroom a democratic setting where everyone feels a responsibility to contribute is a central goal of transformative pedagogy. (p. 93)

Hooks described well the dangers lurking in many classroom feelings:

> I have taught brilliant students of color, many of them seniors, who have skillfully managed to never speak in classroom setttings. Some express the feeling that they are less likely to suffer any kind of assault if they simply do not assert their subjectivity. They have told me that many professors never showed any interest in hearing their voices. Accepting the decentering of the West globally, embracing multiculturalism, compels educators to focus attention on the issue of voice. Who speaks? Who listens? And why? (p. 94)

Those who teach in the multicultural classroom know that what frequently occurs is a form of competition among groups. There is a tendency to see each form of oppression discussed, in light of one's own form of oppression. Hence, there seems to be competition in the form of whose oppression is the worse. The art of the faculty member in translating what one spokesperson for a group is saying to others is significant. Nurturing border crossings becomes imperative for the classroom teacher. The instructor must become a translator of culture (a go-between). In many ways, it is important for the instructor to have the skills necessary to become what Reich (1992) refers to as a "strategic broker." Hooks (1993) succeeds as a strategic broker in crossing borders through what she calls learning different "cultural codes" (p. 95).

In a multicultural classroom it becomes essential then to turn to what Giroux (1992a) has called "border pedagogy" to try and make certain many speak and are heard. According to Giroux, border pedagogy opens a discourse that links the schooling to radical democratic society. Giroux describes border pedagogy as "a language in which one speaks *with* rather than exclusively *for* others" (p. 29, emphasis in original). However, enabling diverse students to speak is not always as pleasurable as one would hope. Once they find their voices, a number have very negative things to say; what frequently occurs seems to be painful as students find their voice and cross cultures and paradigms and become exposed to different kinds of knowing. Frequently, it is hard for one student to represent his or her total group. Too often this occurs as some groups still tend to be few in number. There is always the danger of tokenism, and all too frequently too much is expected from one representative of a group. Ultimately, in the multicultural classroom, growth may not occur for some time and many a professor does not get a chance to see the benefits of his or her teaching within an academic semester.

Despite some of the negatives related to focusing on problems of border and critical pedagogy, the rewards are very substantial to the student and to the faculty member. Unfortunately, there has been a "neglect of pedagogy" in education, schools, and colleges (Gore, 1993)—institutions that should place pedagogy as central. This neglect is not good for our teachers and administrators in their preparation nor is it good for those of us who are faculty. Making explicit not only what we teach but how we teach it enables us to really begin to deal critically with the crucial issues of empowerment and power, oppression and repression, and politics and privilege. In facing up to the realities within our classroom, we will also begin to realize how what we do within the classroom impacts directly on our students and indirectly on society. Critical reflection and dialogue about our teaching can lead to change. Through this reflection and dialogue, our own privileged position of teacher and/or educational leader will become clear, and through this process, we will have more understanding of our own roles in the classroom and we should be better able to empower those we teach.

EMANCIPATORY ACTION RESEARCH AND DIVERSITY

> The "objects" of action research—the things that action researchers research and that they aim to improve—are their own educational practices, their understandings of these practices, and the situations in which they practice. (Carr and Kemmis, 1986, p. 180)

Diverse forms of assessment, self-critical reflection, knowledge bases related to diversity, and diverse pedagogical approaches will not achieve all the needed changes in education. Another approach that may assist in the change process is action research that has proven over time to be very liberating. As coined by Carr and Kemmis (1986), one form of action research is even called emancipatory action research. This term has been given because it empowers teachers and administrators to become the researchers in their own classrooms and schools. It pulls together the critical reflection, that is the essence of critical pedagogy, and it enables educators to have their voices heard beyond the classroom and school walls. It empowers groups of educators to work together on meaningful research, and it speaks to them in languages that are understandable and helpful. There is no credibility or validity problem with such research. Because it is problem centered, it meets real needs and is site specific. And yet when shared with other educators, often it hits a familiar chord and experiences do cross over. Emancipatory action research empowers educators and places them at the center of their own improvement.

Action research first appeared in the works of Lewin (1952) who named the concept in his classic article entitled, ''Group Decisions and Social Change.'' Underlying Lewin's form of action research was a spiral of planning, acting, observing, and reflecting. Action was not seen as an end in itself unless self-reflection continued to occur. Lewin's work introduced the participatory, democratic, and social change concepts that are so much a part of action research today. His research was based in reality focusing on such investigations as discrimination in minority groups, habits of buying foods, or production in factories. Lewin's work took into account two essential aims of action research: to improve and to involve (Adelman, 1993). Although popular for some twenty years in the United States, in the 1970s it began to decline. Carr and Kemmis attribute this to the focus on the research-development-diffusion model that took over in the post-Sputnik era.

However, in the United Kingdom in the 1970s, action research continued as part of the naturalistic research tradition and retained its viability in relation to schools affilitated with the Ford Teaching Project (1973–1976) directed by Elliott and Adelman. The Ford Teaching Project asked teachers, school administrators, and university faculty to become collaborators on action research projects (Elliott, 1985). This work was also linked to the writings of Stenhouse (1975, 1985), who coined the concept of teacher as researcher. Classroom investigations through inquiry were at the heart of the Ford Teaching Project. In this project, school teachers and university faculty conducted research and shared their ideas through the *Classroom Action Research Network*–a series of bulletins produced by the network. Through this network, teachers from all over the United Kingdom linked together to share their ideas through the Center for Applied Research in Education, located at the Cambridge Institute of Education. East Anglia, with MacDonald (1973), Simons (1971), and Stenhouse (1975), was another location to be considered as the East Anglia Center for Applied Research in Education looked to the naturalistic tradition and focused on case study research and evaluation, which complemented the work going on in action research. But it was not only in the United Kingdom where action research with a focus on teacher research began to flourish. The University of Deakin in Australia was another center for this concept and for this kind of research.

Turning to the United States once more, Carini (1975, 1986), at the

Prospect Center and School in Bennington, Vermont, created something very much like action research. This concept took hold despite the research-development-diffusion model, and many examples of this type of research began to flourish, as seen in the writings of Bissex and Bullock (1987), Cochran-Smith and Lytle (1993), Goswami and Stillman (1987), and Mohr and Maclean (1987).

Action research has been defined in many ways. For example, Boomer (1987) defined it as "deliberate, group or personally owned and conducted, solution-oriented investigation" (p. 8).

Cohen and Manion (1984) have given this type of research certain properties:

> –action research is *situational*–it is concerned with diagnosing a problem in specific context and attempting to solve it in that context; it is usually (though not inevitably) *collaborative*–teams of researchers and practitioners work together on a project; it is *participatory*–team members themselves take part directly or indirectly in inplementing the research; and it is *self-evaluative*–modifications are continuously evaluated within the ongoing situation, the ultimate objective being to improve practice in some way or other. (pp. 41–42, emphasis in original)

Its situational, collaborative, participatory, and self-evaluative aspects make action research quite different from traditional, quantitative research. This type of research is carried out with the subjects of the study and is not research done on them.

Unlike Bissex and Bullock (1987), Cochran-Smith and Lytle (1993), and Mohr and Maclean (1987), we have chosen to call this research, action research rather than teacher research in an effort to be more inclusive. If we are to have a "community of thinkers," as Boomer (1987) desires, we need to have not only teachers but also be open to the inclusion of school administrators, school counselors, staff, students, and even parents and school board representatives carrying out research. Action research enables a school administrator, for example, to actually deal with a difficult problem through inquiry. It also asks university researchers to work side-by-side with teachers and focus on their questions rather than privileging one's own (Shapiro, Parssinen, and Brown, 1992). In this way, distancing occurs removing some of the emotions from the situation. Such research also tends to be empowering.

For students, action research can also be liberating enabling them to distance themselves from the difficult problems of learning and growing up. One way to accomplish this is to have students deal with meaningful problems through journal entries, projects, essays, and other important ways. Therefore, action research means not only "reclaiming the classroom" (Goswami and Stillman, 1987) but also reclaiming the school as a focus for inquiry. In this way, the voices of diverse groups will be heard as they seek to answer questions of importance to them related to education. No longer is the university researcher privileged, but many others have a voice in the investigative process and product.

The focus on collaborative research is of special interest. For too long, teachers' and school administrators' doors have been closed. Through collaborative action research, teams of practitioners and even students can work together on common educational problems. They can share questions and seek the answers together. Their findings will be of benefit not only to them but also to their community and possibly society as well.

The liberatory aspect of action research is most important to us. There is something very empowering about carrying out one's own research, finding solutions, and presenting the results to others. Emancipatory action research, as defined by Carr and Kemmis (1986), has the ability to free those who have felt somewhat powerless within the system. It forces teachers, school administrators, and university faculty to ask challenging questions related to the educational system and then attempts to do something about them. Instead of leaving change in the hands of politicians, educational researchers, and remote individuals who do not have a sense of what is really going on in classrooms, emancipatory action research places the change process in the hands of those who care and can carry out modifications day by day within the classroom and within the school. The intent is also to create a community of questioners and learners who can share a growing body of action research projects and obtain ideas from each other. The intent is also to break down the hierarchy of schooling and develop a situation in which everyone, including the students, becomes a learner and a researcher. If done right, it can help to set the stage for participatory involvement receptive to democratic values and traditions.

DIVERSITY AND POSTMODERNISM

> For me, a symbol [of postmodernism] is a Bedouin, mounted on a camel and clad in traditional robes, under which he is wearing jeans, with a transistor radio in his hands and an ad for Coca-Cola on the camel's back. I see this as a typical expression of this multicultural era, a signal that an amalgamation of cultures is taking place. I see it as proof that something is happening, something is being born, that we are in phase when one age

is succeeding another, when everything is possible. (Vaclav Havel, from a speech given on the occasion of receiving the Liberty Medal, as reprinted in the *Philadelphia Inquirer,* July 6, 1994)

The growing trend in American education to broaden the curriculum to include multicultural influences (which we view as an important, though partial, aspect of diversity) is often explained as the outcome of the increasingly multicultural nature of the American population in general, and the student population of American schools in particular. There can be little question that the shifting demographics of education has forced issues of diversity to the forefront. Clearly, as the number of students of color have increased, and as the influence of other previously silenced groups (e.g., women, the disabled, gays and lesbians) has become more pronounced, the curriculum of American schools would have to reflect, at least in part, these changes. We have already presented several perspectives in this chapter on how diversity is affecting education with our discussions of autobiography, pedagogy, changing knowledge bases, and action research. In this section of the chapter we want to focus on a philosophical movement that is affecting many aspects of academic life, including the theoretical foundation of modern educational theory. This is a movement that is generally termed postmodernism and seems like a logical topic to include in a book of this type.

Although the demographic transformation of American schools is undoubtedly a significant cause of the rise of diversity as a basis for curricular reform, we believe that postmodernism is also involved, perhaps causally, but certainly correlationally, in the development of this movement throughout American education. We have used this term at various places throughout the book because any presentation of current trends has to include some mention of postmodernism, even if the writers are against what this movement believes. (Some writers use the term poststructuralism in more or less the same way that postmodernism is used. We will use the latter term in this book because it seems to be the more commonly accepted label.) While an even cursory presentation of postmodernism is beyond the scope of this book, we believe readers of this volume should know enough about this movement to understand its impact on current educational thought. More to the point, postmodernism is a school of thought that is not only consistent with an interest in diversity, it may be one of the reasons why this trend exists.

As a movement in 20th century thought, postmodernism has affected disciplines as wide ranging as art, architecture, literary criticism, and psychology. In his review, Gergen (1994) traces the roots of the movement to Wittgenstein's *Philosophical Investigations* (1963) in which it is proposed that language has meaning through its connections with social practices, not through its reference to an external reality: "To use a word accurately is to use it within the rules of culturally specific language games, in which games are embedded within broader cultural conventions or forms of life. It is not the world as it is that constitutes our callings but the relationships in which we participate" (Gergen, 1994, p. 413). Gergen traces the movement through Rorty's (1979) work asking philosophers to cease looking for transcendent truth and "to begin to participate pragmatically in the broader dialogues of society" (p. 413), and through the writings of Foucault (1978) and Derrida (1953) who believe that knowledge and power are inescapably intertwined.

Although there are many defining aspects of postmodernism, the central tenet that has been brought into education is its vehement attack on positivism. The positivist school of thought is often traced to Auguste Comte's *Positivism,* which was published in 1830. Compte believed that science would solve all of the world's problems by removing all doubts about what was real and what was not real. In positivism, all facts about reality are based on sense data and all laws of science are reducible to empirical propositions. Once sense data have been exhausted, there is nothing else that can be known about the world or about human beings.

As a school of philosophy, the positivists believed that an objective reality exists and that this reality is governed by laws. The purpose of science is to discover these laws through the use of methods that were based on agreed-upon paradigms. Scientists, in this scheme, were those most able to pursue these laws (or truths) because they were the ones trained in the proper use of the methodologies and techniques by which truth could be discovered. As such, positivism was often linked with empiricism because the collection and analysis of data, derived through valid experimental designs, was the best means to obtain the objectivity that positivism desired. Whatever means were employed, however, the goal of science was to achieve more accurate description of the universe and the laws by which it is governed.

To say this in a way more related to educational research, we do research in education to find out "what works" (to use a term straight out of the center of positivist thought). That is, we attempt to find the best method, the best instructional technique, or the best way to group students (or whatever works), with the idea that there is a best way, which our science will discover and the community of people who care about education will then accept as a discovered truth to be used to improve our schools. This objective knowledge is obtainable, desirable, and communicable. Moreover, it is the legitimate domain of those in the educational community who have been trained and designated as researchers to discover these truths and communicate (or, to use the more common phrase, disseminate) these truths to those lower in the hierarchy (for example, teachers) to improve their practice. Thus, traditional educational research flows in one direction, from the researchers to the practitioners, and is based on the search for objective principles that are context-free and universal.

Postmodernism attacks this central tenet of positivism at its source: There is no objective basis for truth; there is no standpoint or method that is superior to any other; all reality is constructed and one construction of reality is as good as any other; science does not, and cannot, seek objective truth, rather it merely establishes one set of conventions based on power and hegemony.

Bereiter (1994), in a recent article on the implications of postmodernism for educational psychology, makes the following statement:

> It is hard even to imagine what could constitute a plausible defense of some particular standpoint as being objective—that is, free of subjective bias. Nevertheless, we continue using such expressions as ''objectively speaking'' as if they meant something. It is not the denial of objectivity, per se, that sets postmodernists apart; it is their insistence on an array of radical implications stemming from this denial. Some of the implications of this position are that:
>
> 1. Mainstream science has been unmasked and shown to be without foundation.
> 2. There is no real progress in science; there is only change, brought about by power struggles among competing groups.
> 3. Scientific thought or the scientific method (however that might be construed) has no intrinsic merit. It is just the way one highly influential group of people happen to think (or to believe that they think).
> 4. So-called misconceptions are only misconceptions judged from a certain standpoint and are perfectly good conceptions when viewed from other, less imperialistic standpoints.
> 5. What constitutes a fact and what constitutes an adequate explanation of a fact are specific to the folkways of the group. (p. 4)

From a postmodern perspective, many ideas that were considered unacceptable twenty years (or even ten years) ago, are now legitimized.

To cite a few examples: theology, science, and magic are merely alternative models of social knowledge with equal claims to respectability; objectivity in research is neither possible nor desirable; narrative descriptions of personal experience are as valid as any other form of data; traditional research methodology is simply one way of doing science, and in fact, may be more problematic than alternative methodologies, etc.

As we have said, it is beyond the scope of this book to adequately present or attempt to evaluate the impact of postmodernism on educational thought. It some ways, the various claims of these writers might seem to those involved in the day-to-day process of providing education to students to be nothing more than another meaningless academic game. Certainly, postmodernism has its critics (see, for example, Smith, 1994), and some of its proponents have carried their arguments beyond reasonable limits. Despite this, it can be argued that this movement has opened the door (or, as some would say, has kicked open the door) to allow alternate points of view to be presented and to permit long-silenced voices to be heard. It is this link to diversity that we find valuable in the context of this book.

In asserting that traditional science, and, in fact, traditional academic pursuits of many types, represent male, white, Eurocentric views of reality, the postmodernists have laid siege to one of the core assumptions in American education—that the accumulation of knowledge is the cornerstone of academic achievement. From this assumption, a host of additional assumptions have always immediately followed—that the curriculum of American schools should consist of the essential elements of knowledge in any field; that this knowledge should be arranged and presented in a hierarchical and sequential fashion that parallels the movement toward a more complete understanding of the truth; that the assessment of how much knowledge a particular student has attained should be the basis for critical educational decisions about that student; that product should take precedence over process, etc. If, however, it is possible to question the very concept of knowledge, at least as something universal and context-free, and if it is acceptable to believe that knowledge consists of agreed-upon conventions that are accepted by a community of people who share a common language and that are generated through interaction and discourse, then most of the core assumptions listed above are brought into doubt. It no longer follows, for example, that there is an essential body of knowledge that should constitute the curriculum of American schools, nor is it reasonable to look for the one best method or the one correct technique to teach this knowledge. In addition, most of our traditional assumptions about assessment are no longer viable, a point that captures many of the important issues in this debate.

If we move away from the notion that education consists of the acquisition of facts (or knowledges, or truths), then it is no longer acceptable to imagine educational assessment as consisting of test items that tap the acquisition of knowledge and for which there is always one correct answer. This point has been made cogently in a recent article by Delandshere and Petrosky (1994).

> Traditionally, essentialists, or positivists, think of knowledge as truths or information that one possesses in a particular subject or field. The more information a person "acquires," the more knowledgeable the person becomes. Knowledge in this sense is a collection of discrete instances of truths or information, identified categorically in subjects or fields that are assumed to be historically linear, progressive, and additive accumulations of concepts, truths and information. Assessments created in the spirit of essentialist notions of knowledge attempt to find out what people know by asking them to reproduce or recognize truths or appropriate information. This kind of thinking values assessment exercises that lead to true or right answers rather than "ill structured" tasks that lead to performances for which there are no single right answers or algorithms for arriving at answers. (pp. 11–12)

These authors relate how a postmodern perspective of knowledge inevitably changes the way we assess educational attainment and provide a case study of how these implications were used in the creation of a new testing system for English and language arts teachers. This case study is also instructive in showing how the desire for standardization, replication, and consistency clash with the revised concept of knowledge, which is inherent in the postmodern school.

In summary, postmodernism is a philosophical movement whose influence is beginning to be felt in education and whose future impact seems potentially immense. We have mentioned some of the implications that we perceive for this movement in the preceding section. Overall, however, we are struck that almost all of the implications of postmodernism for education are identical to those that follow from a belief in diversity. Both positions lead us to ask questions in new ways; both not only allow but demand that different voices must be heard; both challenge the assumption that any educational problem can be solved through a single solution. Whether the relationship between postmodernism and diversity is causal or merely relational, it is striking that both movements lead to almost identical educational prescriptions and have done so at almost exactly the same point in time.

SOCIAL RECONSTRUCTION AND DIVERSITY

> . . . Nonetheless, teachers are unlikely to teach students effectively if they blame them instead of society for their condition. What characterizes these expert teachers is that they understand the structural conditions, but are not totally overwhelmed by them. And despite the limitations imposed by the schools and larger society, they have been able to fashion a teaching philosophy and pedagogy that enables them to act as social agents in ways that both change and construct their own and their pupils' realities. (Foster, 1992, p. 197)

Throughout this book, although not explicitly stated, but implied, we are asking teachers, school leaders, and all other educators to become the social agents whom Foster described in the quotation above. We are asking that all of us become cognizant of the realities in the outside society (i.e., drugs, weapons, abuse, toxicity, dysfunctional families) but that we stop the constant blame and feelings of helplessness that often come when we view those realities, and in so doing, empower ourselves and the next generation as well. Within our own circle, whether it be the classroom, school, or local community, the intention is that we can make a difference and that those we educate can make even greater changes. Starting with self, moving to a study of others, walking in others' shoes, and learning to be critical, can set the stage for movement towards "a language of possibilities" (Giroux, 1992b) and towards action. Like Giroux, we believe it is essential to move towards the empowerment of diverse groups to enable them to see, explore, and develop their own possibilities and those that the society offers them. Social reconstructionism is a concept that has been used to empower groups who have been oppressed.

Brameld (1956) introduced the social reconstructionist approach as a "utopian philosophy." However, over time, this utopian vision has been made more concrete and possible through the writings of scholars such as Aronowitz and Giroux (1985). This movement has also been called conscientization (Freire, 1970), emancipatory pedagogy (Gordon, 1985; Lather, 1991), critical teaching (Shor, 1980), and socialist feminism (Jaggar, 1983; Harraway, 1985). In other contexts it has been referred to as multicultural education (Suzuki, 1984) or antiracist teaching (Carby, 1982; Murrell, 1991).

This antiracist, multicultural, or social reconstructionist approach turns to the work of critical theorists (i.e., Anyon, 1987; Apple, 1986), cognitive development theorists (i.e., Dewey, 1938; Piaget, 1952), and cultural theorists (i.e., Kanter, 1977; Suzuki, 1984). According to Sleeter and Grant (1988), this approach has asked that democratic ideals be practiced in the schools. Sleeter and Grant wrote,

> Practicing democracy also means learning to articulate one's interests, openly debate issues with one's peers, organize and work collectively with others, acquire power, exercise power, and so forth. (p. 187)

Further, Sleeter and Grant add that for oppressed ethnic groups, it has meant

> they must also develop a sense of political efficacy, and be given practice in social action strategies which teaches them how to get power without violence and further exclusion. . . . Opportunities for social action, in which students have experience in obtaining and exercising power, should be emphasized within a curriculum that is designed to help liberate excluded ethnic groups. (p. 149)

Paulo Freire (1970) has used social reconstructionism as a way to teach students (in poor, oppressed, and oppressive countries) to organize themselves for action and not passively obey. Freire's philosophical praxis has found a home, not only in Brazil and Cuba but also in the United States as well (Lankshear and McLaren, 1993; McLaren and Leonard, 1993).

Freire's philosophy and praxis required students, for example, to learn about social action skills. These skills prepared them to focus on democracy with an emphasis on issues of social inequality and injustice. Through social action skills, students learned about ways to organize an election campaign or means to guide decisions through committee procedures.

In Freire's work, action research projects have been frequently used to help awaken the consciousness of those who carry out the project as well as of those who are the subjects and interviewees of the project (Anyon, 1987; Banks, 1991). According to Freire and others, these skills can lead to an awakening of political interest and can indicate to different groups that a collective effort may lead to change within society.

Not only does social reconstructionism, as defined by Freire, turn to group action and action research, but there is also an emphasis in this literature on self-analysis for action. Sleeter and Grant (1988) have advocated the use of students' autobiographies as ways to help themselves and others. Through analysis of their own lives and analysis of critical incidences that have shaped them thus far, Sleeter and Grant and many others believe that the difficult barriers between self and other can be destroyed. Rather than silencing students (Fine, 1989; Weiss and Fine, 1993), there needs to be a discussion of crucial decisions made in people's lives that include the difficult topics of having a baby, dropping out of school, or taking drugs (Aronowitz and Giroux, 1985). Such discussions, if approached with care, have the potential to empower young people and indicate the importance of life choices and options.

In his writings and lectures, Giroux (1992b) speaks of teachers as transformative intellectuals. By this he means that teachers as well as other educators should be engaged in solving societal problems and they should encourage their students to do the same. In discussing this vision for teachers, Giroux stated in an interview,

> They do not operate from an aloof perspective that legitimizes the separation of facts from values. They understand the nature of their own self-formation, have some vision of the future, see the importance of education as a public discourse, and have a sense of mission in providing students what they need to become critical citizens. So to give you a somewhat schematic sense of what I mean by teachers as transformative intellectuals, I would say, first that teachers are engaged. They are partisans, not doctrinaire. They believe something, say what they believe, and offer their beliefs to others in a framework that always makes it debatable and open to critical inquiry. Second, to talk about teachers as intellectuals is to say they should have an active role in shaping the curriculum. (pp. 20–21)

The preceding suggestions and the concept of teachers as intellectuals, based on the social reconstructionist approach, are just some of the ways to move towards revised knowledge bases and transformed curricula for teacher education and for school administrative preparation. Such suggestions can empower teachers as well as administrators and can in turn lead to the empowerment of their students. In so doing, the voices of many different groups will be heard and respected, and the culture of the community and the school will be more in harmony with each other.

Although focused only on teacher education, Sleeter (1992) expressed her thoughts regarding social reconstructionism and empowerment this way

> Ultimately, teacher education programs that are rooted in a radical structuralist analysis of oppression should help teachers develop links with local collective actions aimed at challenging oppression and help

> teachers develop both teaching practices and organized pressure activities that will advance the interest of oppressed people. (p. 41)

But the road towards social reconstructionism is a bumpy one. There are deep potholes on the way. For example, groups do not move together in a lock step way. There is a nonsynchronous position of groups (McCarthy and Apple, 1988) that leads to an asymmetry or nonparallelism (Hicks, 1981) among the groups. This can occur when economic and political needs may not be the same for a given group as for another at a particular point in time. There may also be rivalry between and among groups because of the few resources available to all and the need to fight for them in competitive ways. Divide and conquer has been effectively practiced for a long time and it is hard to change that approach. Hence, group rivalry may occur and this may lead to resistance and reluctance towards change. How to create an empathy of one group towards another as well as eventually bring about a win/win situation, is far from easy. And yet, the positives far outweigh the negatives.

To avoid nonsynchrony, Sleeter (1991) has encouraged the merging of multiculturalism and social reconstructionism. She has indicated that this combination "forges a coalition among various oppressed groups as well as members of dominant groups, teaching directly about political and economic oppression and discrimination, and preparing young people directly in social action skills" (p. 12). Such a combination has the potential to be forceful and empowering.

The movement towards social reconstruction merged with diversity should be ongoing and it should be challenging. Although not directly addressing the concept of diversity, the social reconstructionist movement, and implicitly the multicultural movement, have been summarized well by Capper (1993) when she wrote,

> Thus, continuous school renewal suggests the incessant process of constructing, deconstructing, and reconstructing what we do as educators—in our classrooms, schools, districts, communities, and universities—in the name of meaningful education for all students for the purpose of advancing a democratic society. (p. 290)

CONCLUSION

Throughout this book, we have been attempting to create a process similar to that described by Capper. We have been asking ourselves—the three of us and you, the reader—to try to construct, deconstruct, and reconstruct our lives, our work, and even our society. The process we have designed need not be carried out in a lock step fashion; however we have taken you on our own journey of self-discovery in which we first turned to autobiography, with a focus on critical incidences that awakened each of us to categories of difference. We then embarked upon a quest for a model that might encompass our individual and current view of diversity and education. We presented a few models relating to diversity, one of which showed diversity as more of an additive model in which we continued to add on a layer of difference as we opened our eyes to another aspect of diversity. We also presented some dynamic models of diversity that displayed intersections of one or more aspects of diversity with other categories of difference over time.

Once we began to work out who we were and how we viewed the diverse world in which we now exist, we asked that all of us look at whom we teach or work with and help the others (i.e., students, clients, staff) get a sense of self. We suggested that reading widely in appropriate knowledge bases in areas related to differences in kind (i.e., sex/gender, social class, sexual diversity, race/ethnicity) and to differences in degree (i.e., learning styles, multiple intelligences, learning disabilities, giftedness) would be helpful. Finally, we turned to other issues related to diversity that impinge on our understanding of this complex area and our ability to deal with and appreciate difference (i.e., diverse assessment, varied pedagogies, emancipatory action research, postmodernism, social reconstructionism).

In the prologue of this book, we indicated that we did not find the writing of this manuscript to be easy. Throughout we have had some difficult dialogues. We have still not reached a consensus on a number of issues related to diversity. However, we have realized that we need not agree on all aspects of diversity to work together, learn, and grow. Nevertheless, despite our continued differences, we do agree on some essentials – that we must provide high quality education for all children, irrespective of their gender, race/ethnicity, social class, and other areas of difference; and that we should prepare all of our young people for a pluralistic, democratic society in which they can participate by finding their voices. To achieve these objectives, we strongly feel that diverse students must be perceived by educators not as problems but as offering a world full of possibilities. The writing of this book has inspired us to continue our own journey in understanding and respecting the complex area of diversity. We hope that we have inspired you to construct, deconstruct, and reconstruct self, others, and schooling for the 21st century.

The Multicultural Education Infusion Center

THE PURPOSE OF the Multicultural Education Infusion Center (MEIC) is to increase the capability of Colleges and Schools of Education to prepare teacher educators for a multicultural and linguistically diverse student population. The center provides professional development opportunities for faculty and administrators to expand their knowledge and understanding of research-based strategies that improve the learning of culturally diverse and limited English proficient K–12 students. The MEIC also assists participating institutions in planning and implementing fundamental, systemic change that will facilitate the infusion of multicultural/multilingual education into their curricula.

To accomplish these goals, the MEIC has formed a national partnership with twenty-three schools and colleges of education that are committed to serving the needs of diverse learners. These institutions comprise a continuing network whose members offer mutual support, receive technical assistance from the center, and provide technical assistance to colleges and universities within their regions.

The MEIC provides an intensive two-week residential Summer Institute to teams of three to four faculty and administrators from each participating institution. Through the Institute, participants increase their understanding of frameworks for multicultural and multilingual education; characteristics of diverse group and implications for learning; effective strategies for second language learners; and applications to content area instruction. Additionally, the Summer Institute supports development of organizational change strategies; personal and institutional action plans for promoting transformation; and approaches to course revision for multicultural infusion. Institute activities involve participants in discussions with nationally recognized experts in multicultural and multilingual education, small-group planning and problem solving, field trips to exemplary sites, cultural events, and networking.

Participating institutions increasingly contribute their knowledge and expertise to network colleagues and other universities. The center and members continue to share information through a newsletter; meetings at professional conferences; and regional meetings for faculty development.

The MEIC is funded through a grant from the U.S. Office of Bilingual Education and Minority Language Affairs. Dr. Ann I. Morey and Dr. Margie K. Kitano are Director and Associate Director of the MEIC respectively. Additionally, Dr. Morey is Dean and Dr. Kitano is Associate Dean of San Diego State University's College of Education.

BIBLIOGRAPHY

AAUW. 1991. *Stalled Agenda: Gender Equity and the Training of Educators*. Washington, DC: Educational Foundation and National Education Association.

AAUW. 1992. *How Schools Shortchange Girls: A Study of Major Findings on Girls and Education*. Washington, DC: Educational Foundation and National Education Association.

Abbey, A. and C. Melby. 1986. "The Effects of Nonverbal Cues on Gender Differences in Perceptions of Sexual Intent," *Sex Roles*, 15(5/6):283–298.

Ada, A. F. 1988. "The Pajaro Valley Experience: Working with Spanish-Speaking Parents to Develop Children's Reading and Writing Skills in the Home through the Use of Children's Literature," in *Minority Education: From Shame to Struggle*, T. Skutnabb-Kangas and J. Cummins, eds., Clevedon, England: Multilingual Matters.

Adam, B. 1987. *The Rise of a Gay Liberation Movement*. Boston, MA: Twayne.

Adams, K. 1990. "Examining Black Underrepresentation in Gifted Programs," paper presented at the *Annual Meeting of the National Association for Gifted Education*, New Orleans LA.

Adelman, C. 1993. "Kurt Lewin and the Origins of Action Research," *Educational Action Research*, 1(1):7–24.

Aiken, S. H., K. Anderson, M. Dinnerstein, J. Lensink and P. MacCorquodale. 1987. "Trying Transformations: Curriculum Integration and the Problem of Resistance," *SIGNS: Journal of Women Culture and Society*, 12:255–275.

Allport, F. H. 1924. *Social Psychology*. Boston, MA: Houghton-Mifflin.

American Psychiatric Association. 1980. *Diagnostic and Statistical Manual of Menial Disorders*. Third edition. Washington, DC: American Psychiatric Association.

Anderson, M. L. 1988. *Thinking about Women: Sociological Perspectives on Sex and Gender*. New York, NY: Macmillan.

Anyon, J. 1987. "Social Class and School Knowledge," *Curriculum Inquiry*, 11:3–42.

Apple, M. W., ed. 1982. *Cultural and Economic Reproduction in Education: Essays on Class, Ideology and the State*. London, England: Routledge & Kegan Paul.

Apple, M. W. 1986. *Teachers and Texts: A Political Economy of Class and Gender Relations in Education*. New York, NY: Routledge & Kegan Paul.

Arch, E. C., S. E. Kirschner and M. K. Tetreault. "Measuring the Impact of Faculty Development in Women's Studies," paper presented at *The Annual Conference of the National Women's Studies Association*, Humboldt, CA, 1983 (unpublished).

Archer, J. and B. Lloyd. 1989. *Sex and Gender.* London, England: Cambridge University Press.

Aronowitz, S. and H. Giroux. 1985. *Education under Siege.* S. Hadley, MA: Bergin & Garvey.

Asante, M. K. 1987. *The Afrocentric Idea.* Philadelphia, PA: Temple University Press.

Asante, M. K. 1991–1992. "Afrocentric Curriculum," *Educational Leadership,* 49(4):28–31.

Ashton-Warner, S. 1963. *Teacher.* New York, NY: Simon and Schuster.

Association for Supervision and Curriculum Development (ASCD). 1990. *Resolutions 1990.* Alexandria, VA: ASCD.

Au, K. H. and C. Jordan. 1980. "Teaching Reading to Hawaiian Children: Finding a Culturally Appropriate Solution," in *Culture in the Bilingual Classroom,* H. Trueba, G. P. Guthrie and K. H. Au, eds., Rowley, MA: Newbury House.

August, D. and E. Garcia. 1988. *Language Minority Education in the United States: Research, Policy and Practice.* Chicago, IL: Charles C. Thomas.

Ayers, W. 1992. "Teachers' Stories: Autobiography and Inquiry," in *Teacher Personal Theorizing: Connecting Curriculum Practice, Theory, and Research,* E. W. Ross, J. W. Cornett and G. McCutcheon, eds., Albany, NY: State University of New York Press, pp. 35–49.

Balthazor, M. J., R. K. Wagner and W. E. Pelham. 1991. "The Specificity of the Effects of Stimulant Medication on Classroom Learning-Related Measures of Cognitive Processing for Attention Deficit Disorder Children," *Journal of Abnormal Child Psychology,* 19(1):35–52.

Banks, J. A. 1991. *Teaching Strategies for Ethnic Studies.* Fifth edition. Boston, MA: Allyn and Bacon.

Banks, J. A. and C. A. Banks. 1993. *Multicultural Education: Issues and Perspectives.* Second edition. Boston, MA: Allyn and Bacon.

Beauchamp, T. L. and J. F. Childress. 1984. "Morality, Ethics, and Ethical Theories," in *Ethics, Education and Administrative Decisions: A Book of Readings,* P. A. Sola, ed., New York, NY: Peter Lang, pp. 39–65.

Beck, L. G. 1994. *Reclaiming Educational Administration as a Caring Profession.* New York, NY: Teachers College Press.

Belanoff, P. and M. Dickson, eds. 1991. *Portfolios: Process and Product.* Portsmouth, NH: Boynton/Cook.

Belenky, M. F., B. M. Clinchy, N. R. Goldberger and J. M. Tarule. 1986. *Women's Ways of Knowing: The Development of Self, Voice, and Mind.* New York, NY: Basic Books.

BenShalom vs. *Marsh.* 1988. 690 F. Spp.774,777 (E.D. Wis. 1988).

Bereiter, C. 1994. "Implications of Postmodernism for Science, or, Science as Progressive Discourse," *Educational Psychologist,* 29(1):3–12.

Berger, P. L. 1963. *Invitation to Sociology.* Garden City, NJ: Anchor Books.

Bernstein, B. 1982. "Codes, Modalities and the Process of Cultural Reproduction: A Model," in *Cultural and Economic Reproduction in Education,* M. W. Apple, ed., London, England: Routledge and Kegan Paul, pp. 304–354.

Biemiller, A. 1993. "Lake Wobegon Revisited: On Diversity and Education," *Educational Researcher,* 22(9):7–12.

Bissex, G. and R. Bullock. 1987. *Seeing for Ourselves: Case Study Research by Teachers of Writing.* Portsmouth, NH: Heinemann.

Blau, P. M. and O. D. Duncan. 1967. *The American Occupational Structure.* New York, NY: John Wiley.

Bloom, B. 1984. "The Search for Methods of Group Instruction as Effective as One-to-One Tutoring," *Educational Leadership,* 41(8):4–17.

Bly, R. 1981. *The Man in the Black Coat Turns.* New York, NY: Doubleday.

Bolman, L. G. and T. E. Deal. 1991. *Reframing Organizations: Artistry, Choice, and Leadership.* San Francisco, CA: Jossey-Bass.

Boomer, G. 1987. "Addressing the Problem of Elsewhereness: A Case for Action Research in Schools," in *Reclaiming the Classroom: Teacher Research as an Agency for Change,* D. Goswami and P. Stillman, eds., Upper Montclair, NJ: Boynton/Cook, pp. 4–12.

Bourdieu, P. 1977. "Cultural Reproduction and Social Reproduction," in *Power and Ideology in Education,* J. Karabel and A. H. Halsey, eds., New York, NY: Oxford, pp. 487–511.

Bourdieu, P. 1984. *Distinction: A Social Critique of the Judgment of Taste.* Translated by R. Nice. Cambridge, MA: Harvard University Press.

Bowers, C. A. and D. J. Flinders. 1990. *Responsive Teaching: An Ecological Approach to Classroom Patterns of Language, Culture, and Thought.* New York, NY: Teachers College Press.

Bowles, S. and H. Gintis. 1976. *Schooling in Capitalist America.* New York, NY: Basic Books.

Brameld, T. B. H. 1956. *Toward a Reconstructed Philosophy of Education.* New York, NY: Holt, Rinehart and Winston.

Braxton, J. M. 1989. *Black Women Writing Autobiography: A Tradition within a Tradition.* Philadelphia, PA: Temple University Press.

Brown, L. and N. Hoffman, eds. 1991. "Women, Girls and the Culture of Education, *Women's Studies Quarterly,* (Special Issue) 19(1 and 2):1–178.

Bullivant, B. M. 1989. "Culture: Its Nature and Meaning for Educators," in *Multicultural Education: Issues and Perspectives,* J. A. Banks and C. A. McGee Banks, eds., Boston, MA: Allyn and Bacon, pp. 27–48.

Burleson, D. L., ed. 1991. *Reflections: Personal Essays by 33 Distinguished Educators.* Bloomington, IN: Phi Delta Kappa.

Camp, R. 1990. "Thinking Together about Portfolios," *The Quarterly of the National Writing Project and the Center for the Study of Writing,* 12(2):8–24.

Candelaria, N. 1993. "The Day the Cisco Kid Shot John Wayne," in *Growing Up Latino: Memories and Stories,* H. Augenbraum and I. Stavans, eds., Boston, MA: Houghton Mifflin, pp. 115–130.

Capper, C. A., ed. 1993. *Educational Administration in a Pluralistic Society.* Albany, NY: State University of New York.

Carbo, M. 1981. "Grades 3–12: An Adaptation of the Learning Style Inventory," *Reading Style Inventory,* Englewood Cliffs, NJ: Prentice-Hall.

Carbo, M., R. Dunn and K. Dunn. 1986. *Teaching Students to Read through Their Individual Learning Styles.* Englewood Cliffs, NJ: Prentice-Hall.

Carby, H. 1982. "Schooling in Babylon," in Center for Contemporary Cultural Studies,

The Empire Strikes Back: Race and Racism in 70's Britain. Wolfeboro, NH: Longwood, pp. 183–211.

Carini, P. 1975. *The Art of Seeing and the Visibility of the Person.* Grand Forks, ND: University of North Dakota.

Carini, P. 1986. *Prospect's Documentary Processes.* Bennington, VT: The Prospect School Center.

Carr, W. and S. Kemmis. 1986. *Becoming Critical: Education, Knowledge and Action Research.* London, England: Falmer Press.

Chamberlin, J. G. 1981. *The Educating Act.* Lanham, MD: University Press of America, Ch. 7, p. 177.

Chittenden, E. 1991. "Authentic Assessment, Evaluation, and Documentation of Student Performance," in *Expanding Student Assessment,* V. Perrone, ed., Washington, DC: Association for Supervision and Curriculum Development, pp. 22–31.

Cholakis, M. M. 1986. "An Experimental Investigation of the Relationship between and among Sociological Preferences, Vocabulary Instruction and Achievement, and the Attitudes of New York Urban Seventh and Eighth Grade Underachievers," *Dissertation Abstracts International,* 47(11):4046A.

Clatterbaugh, K. 1990. *Contemporary Perspectives on Masculinity: Men, Women, and Politics in Modern Society.* Boulder, CO: Westview Press.

Cochran-Smith, M. and S. L. Lytle. 1993. *Inside/Outside: Teacher Research and Knowledge.* New York, NY: Teachers College Press.

Cohen, L. and L. Manion. 1984. "Action Research," in *Conducting Small-Scale Investigations in Educational Management,* J. Bell, T. Bush, A. Fox, J. Goodey and S. Goulding, eds., London, England: Harper and Row, pp. 41–71.

Cohen, S. B., A. M. Landa and J. M. Tarule. 1990. *The Collaborative Learning Assessment Packet.* Cambridge, MA: Lesley College.

Cohen, S. A., J. S. Hyman, L. Ashcroft and D. Loveless. 1989. "Mastery Learning versus Learning Styles versus Metacognitives: What Do We Tell the Practitioner?" Paper presented at *The Annual Meeting of the American Educational Research Associates,* San Francisco, CA.

Conroy, P. 1972. *The Water Is Wide.* New York, NY: Bantam.

Cooper, J. E. 1991. "Telling Our Own Stories: The Reading and Writing of Journals or Diaries," in *Stories Lives Tell: Narrative and Dialogue in Education,* C. Witherell and N. Noddings, eds., New York, NY: Teachers College Press, pp. 96–112.

Corno, L. and R. E. Snow. 1986. "Adapting Teaching to Individual Differences among Learners," in *Handbook of Research on Teaching.* Third edition, M. C. Wittrock, ed., New York, NY: Macmillan.

Cortes, C. E. 1986. "The Education of Language Minority Students: A Contextual Interaction Model," in *Beyond Language: Social and Cultural Factors in Schooling Language Minority Students,* California State Department of Education, Los Angeles, CA: California State University, pp. 3–34.

Cramer, R. H. 1991. "The Education of Gifted Children in the United States" *Gifted Child Quarterly,* 35(2):84–91.

Cronbach, L. J. 1975. "Five Decades of Public Controversy over Mental Testing," *American Psychologist,* 30:1–14.

Culley, M. and C. Portuges, eds. 1985. *Gendered Subjects: The Dynamics of Feminist Teaching.* Boston, MA: Routledge & Kegan Paul.

Cummins, J. 1986. "Empowering Minority Students: A Framework for Intervention," *Harvard Educational Review,* 56(1):18–35.

Curry, L. 1990. "Critique of the Research on Learning Styles," *Educational Leadership,* 48(2):50–56.

Cushner, M., A. McClelland and P. Safford. 1992. *Human Diversity in Education: An Integrative Approach.* New York, NY: McGraw Hill.

Darling-Hammond, L. 1991. "The Implications of Testing Policy for Educational Quality and Equality," *Phi Delta Kappan,* 73(3):220–225.

Darling-Hammond, L. 1994. "Performance-Based Assessment and Educational Equity," *Harvard Educational Review,* 64(1):5–29.

Davidson, A. L. and P. Phelan. 1993. "Cultural Diversity and Its Implications for Schooling: A Continuing American Dialogue," in *Renegotiating Cultural Diversity in American Schools,* P. Phelan and A. Locke Davidson, eds., New York, NY: Teachers College Press, pp. 1–26.

DeGregoris, C. N. 1986. "Reading Comprehension and the Interaction of Individual Sound Preferences and Varied Auditory Distractions," *Dissertation Abstracts International,* 47(09):3380A.

Delamont, S. 1983. "The Conservative School? Sex Roles at Home, at Work, and at School," in *Gender, Class and Education,* S. Walker and L. Barton, eds., Sussex: The Falmer Press, pp. 93–106.

Delandshere, G. and A. R. Petrovsky. 1994. "Capturing Teachers' Knowledge: Performance Assessment a) and Post-Structuralist Epistemology; b) From a Post-Structuralist Perspective; c) and Post-Structuralism; d) None of the Above," *Educational Researcher,* 23(5):11–18.

DeLyon, H. and F. Widdowson Migniuolo, eds. 1989. *Women Teachers: Issues and Experiences.* Philadelphia, PA: Open University Press.

Derrida, J. 1953. *Positions.* London, England: Athone Press.

Dewey, J. 1902. *The School and Society.* Chicago, IL: University of Chicago Press.

Dewey, J. 1938. *Experience and Education.* New York, NY: Macmillan.

Dewey, J. 1957. *Reconstruction in Philosophy.* Boston, MA: Beacon Press.

Diamond, J. 1983. *Inside Out: Becoming My Own Man.* San Raphael, CA: Fifth Wave.

Dijkstra, B. 1986. *Idols of Perversity: Fantasies of Feminine Evil in Fin-de-Siecle Culture.* New York, NY: Oxford University Press.

Douglas, C. B. 1979. "Making Biology Easier to Understand," *The American Biology Teacher,* 41(5):277–281, 298–299.

Doyle, J. 1989. *The Male Experience.* Second edition. Dubuque, IA: Wm. C. Brown.

DuCette, J. P., J. P. Shapiro and T. E. Sewell. 1992. "Cultural Diversity, National Testing and the Multicultural Curriculum," paper presented at *The Annual Conference of American Educational Education Association,* San Francisco, CA.

DuCette, J. P., J. P. Shapiro and T. E. Sewell. (in press). "Diversity in Education: Possibilities and Problems," in *A Knowledge Base for Teacher Education,* F. Murray, ed., San Francisco, CA: Jossey-Bass.

Dunn, R., K. Dunn and G. E. Price. 1975, 1979, 1981, 1985. *Learning Style Inventory Manual.* Lawrence, KS: Price Systems.

Dunn, R., J. S. Beaudry and A. Klavas. 1989. "Survey of Research on Learning Styles," *Educational Leadership,* 48(2):50–58.

Dunn, R., J. Gemake, F. Jalali and R. Zenhausern. 1990. "Cross-Cultural Differences in Learning Styles of Elementary-Age Students from Four Ethnic Backgrounds," *Journal of Multicultural Counseling and Development,* 18:68–93.

Dunn, R., J. DellaValle, K. Dunn, G. Geisert, R. Sinatra and R. Zenhausern. 1986. "The Effects of Matching and Mismatching Students' Mobility Preferences on Recognition and Memory Tasks," *Journal of Educational Research,* 79(5):267–272.

Elliott, J. 1985. "Facilitating Action-Research in Schools: Some Dilemmas," in *Field Methods in the Study of Education,* R. G. Burgess, ed., London, England: The Falmer Press, pp. 235–262.

Elliott, R. 1987. *Litigating Intelligence: IQ Tests, Special Education and Social Science in the Courtroom.* Dover, DE: Auburn House Publishing Co.

Ellsworth, E. 1989. "Why Doesn't This Feel Empowering: Working through the Repressive Myths of Critical Pedagogy," *Harvard Educational Review,* 59(3):297–324.

Fauth, G. C. 1984. "Women in Educational Administration: A Research Profile," *The Educational Forum,* 49:65–79.

Feingold, A. 1992. "Sex Differences in Variability in Intellectual Abilities: A New Look at an Old Controversy," *Review of Educational Research,* 62(1):61–84.

Felice, L. G. 1981. "Black Student Dropout Behavior: Disengagement from School Rejection and Racial Discrimination," *Journal of Negro Education,* 50:415–424.

Ferguson, K. E. 1984. *The Feminist Case against Bureaucracy.* Philadelphia, PA: Temple University Press.

Fernback, D. 1981. *The Spiral Path.* Boston, MA: Alyson Publications.

Fine, M. 1989. "Silencing and Nurturing Voice in an Improbable Context: Urban Adolescents in Public School," in *Critical Pedagogy, the State and Cultural Struggle,* H. A. Giroux and P. McLaren, eds., Albany, NY: SUNY, pp. 152–174.

Fine, M. 1991. *Framing Dropouts: Notes on the Politics of Urban High Schools.* Albany, NY: SUNY Press.

Flanagan, C. 1993. "Gender and Social Class: Intersecting Issues in Women's Achievement," *Educational Psychologist,* 28(4):357–378.

Fordham, S. 1988. "Racelessness as a Factor in Black Students' School Success: Pragmatic Strategy or Pyrrhic Victory," *Harvard Educational Review,* 58:54–84.

Foster, M. 1991. " 'Just Got to Find a Way': Case Studies of the Lives and Practice of Exemplary Black High School Teachers," in *Into Schools and Schooling,* M. Foster, ed., New York, NY: AMS Press, pp. 273–309.

Foster, M. 1992. "The Politics of Race," in *What Schools Can Do: Critical Pedagogy and Practice,* K. Weiler and C. Mitchell, eds., Albany, NY: State University of New York Press, pp. 177–202.

Foster, W. 1986. *Paradigms and Promises: New Approaches to Educational Administration.* Buffalo, NY: Prometheus Books.

Foucault, M. 1978. *Language, Counter-Memory, Practice: Selected Essays and Interviews.* Edited by Donald Bouchard. Ithaca, NY: Cornell University Press.

Freire, P. 1970. *Pedagogy of the Oppressed.* New York, NY: Continuum Press.

Freire, P. and I. Shor. 1987. *A Pedagogy for Liberation: Dialogues on Transforming Education.* South Hadley, MA: Bergin and Garvey.

Fritsche, J. A. M. 1984. *Toward Excellence and Equity: The Scholarship on Women as a Catalyst for Change in the University.* Orono, ME: University of Maine.

Fuerstein, R. 1979. *The Dynamic Assessment of Retarded Performances: The Learning Potential Assessment Device, Theory, Instruments and Techniques.* Baltimore, MD: University Park Press, Ch. 6, p. 165.

Fuller, B. and P. Clarke. 1994. "Raising School Effects while Ignoring Culture? Local Conditions and the Influence of Classroom Tools, Rules and Pedagogy," *Review of Educational Research,* 64(1):119–157.

Gabriel, S. L. and I. Smithson, eds. 1990. *Gender in the Classroom: Power and Pedagogy.* Urbana, IL: University of Illinois Press.

Gage, N. L. and D. Berliner. 1991. *Educational Psychology.* Fifth edition. Boston, MA: Houghton Mifflin.

Gallagher, A. M. and R. DeLisi. 1994. "Gender Differences in Scholastic Aptitude Test-Mathematics Problem Solving among High-Ability Students," *Journal of Educational Psychology,* 86(2):204–211.

Garcia, E. E. 1993. "Language, Culture, and Education," in *Review of Research in Education,* L. Darling-Hammond, ed., Washington, DC: American Educational Research Association, pp. 51–98.

Garcia, G. E. and P. D. Pearson. 1994. "Assessment and Diversity" in *Review of Research in Education,* Vol. 20, L. Darling-Hammond, ed., Washington, DC: American Educational Research Association.

Gardner, H. 1983. *Frames of Mind.* New York, NY: Basic Books, Inc.

Gardner, H. and T. Hatch. 1989. "Multiple Intelligences Go to School: Educational Implications of the Theory of Multiple Intelligences," *Educational Researcher,* 18(8):4–10.

Garibaldi, A. M. 1986. "Sustaining Black Educational Progress: Challenges for the 1990's," *Journal of Negro Education,* 55(3):386–396.

Gay, G. 1973. "Racism in America: Imperatives for Teaching Ethnic Studies," in *Teaching Ethnic Studies: Concepts and Strategies,* J. A. Banks, ed., Washington, DC: National Council for Social Studies.

Gay, G. 1994. Personal communication. Discussed at the Multicultural Infusion Network Institute, San Diego, CA, June 14, 1994.

Gehrke, N. J. 1987. *On Being a Teacher.* West Lafayette, IN: Kappa Delta Pi.

Gergen, K. J. 1994. "Exploring the Postmodern: Perils or Potentials?" *American Psychologist,* 49(5):412–416.

Getzels, J. W. and J. T. Dillon. 1973. "The Nature of Giftedness and the Education of the Gifted Child," in *Second Handbook of Research on Teaching,* R. M. W. Travers, ed., Chicago, IL: Rand McNally.

Gibbs, J. T. 1988. *Young, Black and Male in America: An Endangered Species.* Dover, DE: Auburn House.

Gilder, G. 1973. *Sexual Suicide.* New York, NY: Bantam.

Gilder, G. 1986. *Men and Marriage.* New York, NY: Pelican.

Gilligan, C. 1982. *In a Different Voice: Psychological Theory and Women's Development.* Cambridge, MA: Harvard University Press.

Gilligan, C., J. V. Ward and J. M. Taylor. 1988. *Mapping the Moral Domain.* Cambridge, MA: Harvard University.

Giroux, H. A. 1983. "Theories of Reproduction and Resistance in the New Sociology of Education: A Critical Analysis," *Harvard Educational Review,* 53:257–293.

Giroux, H. A., ed. 1991. *Postmodernism, Feminism, and Cultural Politics: Redrawing Educational Boundaries.* Albany, NY: State University of New York Press.

Giroux, H. A. 1992a. *Border Crossings: Cultural Workers and the Politics of Education.* New York, NY: Routledge.

Giroux, H. A. 1992b. "Educational Leadership and the Crisis of Democratic Government," *Educational Researcher,* 20(4):4–11.

Giroux, H. A. 1992c. "The Hope of Radical Education," in *What Schools Can Do: Critical Pedagogy and Practice,* K. Weiler and C. Mitchell, eds., Albany, NY: State University of New York Press, pp. 13–26.

Giroux, H. A. 1994. "Educational Leadership and School Administrators: Rethinking the Meaning of Democratic Public Culture," in *Democratic Leadership: The Changing Context of Administrative Preparation,* T. Mulkeen, N. H. Cambron-McCabe and B. Anderson, eds., Norwood, NJ: Ablex Publishing Company, pp. 31–47.

Goldberg, H. 1987. *The Inner Male: Overcoming Roadblocks to Intimacy.* New York, NY: New American Library.

Gollnick, D. M. and P. C. Chinn. 1994. *Multicultural Education in a Pluralistic Society.* Columbus, OH: Merrill.

Goodlad, J. I. 1990. *Teachers for Our Nations Schools.* San Francisco, CA: Jossey-Bass.

Gordon, B. M. 1982. "Towards a Theory of Knowledge Acquisition for Black Children," *Journal of Education,* 164:90–108.

Gordon, B. M. 1985. "Toward Emancipation in Citizenship Education: The Case of African-American Cultural Knowledge," *Theory and Research in Social Education,* 12:1–23.

Gore, J. M. 1993. *The Struggle for Pedagogies: Critical and Feminist Discourses as Regimes of Truth.* New York, NY: Routledge.

Goswami, D. and P. Stillman. 1987. *Reclaiming the Classroom: Teacher Research as an Agency for Change.* Upper Montclair, NJ: Boynton/Cook.

Gough, H. G. and A. B. Heilbrun. 1965. *Adjective Checklist Manual.* Palo Alto, CA: Consulting Psychologist's Press.

Gould, S. 1981. *The Mismeasure of Man.* New York, NY: Norton.

Grant, C. A. and W. G. Secada. 1991. "Preparing Teachers for Diversity," in *Handbook of Research on Teacher Education,* W. R. Huston, ed., New York, NY: Macmillan.

Greene, M. 1988. *The Dialectic of Freedom.* New York, NY: Teachers College Press.

Greene, M. 1993. "Education, Art, and Mastery: Toward the Spheres of Freedom," in *Critical Social Issues in American Education: Toward the 21st Century,* H. S. Shapiro and D. E. Purpel, eds., New York, NY: Longman, pp. 330–344.

Greenfield, W. D. 1993. "Articulating Values and Ethics in Administrator Preparation," in *Educational Administration in a Pluralistic Society,* C. A. Capper, ed., Albany, NY: State University of New York Press, pp. 267–287.

Grumet, M. 1988. "Supervision and Situation: A Methodology of Self-Report for Teacher Education," *Journal of Curriculum Theorizing,* 1(1):191–257.

Gunter, N. C. and B. G. Gunter. 1990. "The Need for Research," in *Sex Differences in Cognitive Abilities,* D. F. Halpern, ed., Hillsdale, NJ: Lawrence Erlbaum Associates.

Haffner, D. 1990. *Sex Education 2000: A Call to Action.* New York, NY: Sex Information and Education Council of the United States.

Haladyna, T. M., S. B. Nolen and N. S. Haas. 1991. "Raising Standardized Achievement Test Scores and the Origins of Test Score Pollution," *Educational Researcher,* 20(5):2–7.

Hale-Benson, J. E. 1982. *Black Children: Their Roots, Culture, and Learning Style.* Baltimore, MD: Johns Hopkins University Press.

Hall, R. M. and B. Sandler. 1982. *The Classroom Climate: A Chilly One for Women?* Project on the Status and Education of Women. Washington, DC: Association of American Colleges.

Hammill, D. D. 1990. "On Defining Learning Disabilities: Am Emerging Consensus," *Journal of Learning Disabilities,* 23(2):74–84.

Harraway, D. 1985. "A Manifesto for Cyborgs: Science, Technology and Socialist Feminism in the 1980's," *Socialist Review,* 80:65–107.

Harris, A. and S. Carlton. "Pattern of Gender Differences on Mathematics Items on the Scholastic Aptitude Test," paper presented at *The Annual Meeting of the American Educational Research Association,* Boston, MA, 1990 (unpublished).

Heath, S. B. 1982. "What No Bedtime Story Means: Narrative Skills at Home and School," *Language in Society,* 11(1):49–76.

Heath, S. B. 1983. *Way with Words.* Cambridge, England: Cambridge University Press.

Heilbrun, C. 1988. *Writing a Woman's Life.* New York, NY: W. W. Norton.

Henry, A. 1993–1994. "There Are No Safe Places: Pedagogy as Powerful and Dangerous Terrain," *Action in Teacher Education,* XV(4):1–4.

Hernandez, H. 1989. *Multicultural Education: A Teacher's Guide to Content and Process.* Columbus, OH: Merrill.

Herrnstein, R. J. and C. Murray. 1994. *The Bell Curve: Intelligence and Class Structure in American Life.* NY: The Free Press.

Hetrick, B. 1990. "Contingencies Affecting Principal's Management Behavior of Goal Setting," *DAI,* 51:759A.

Hicks, E. 1981. "Cultural Marxism: Nonsynchrony and Feminist Practice," in *Women and Revolution,* L. Sargent, ed., Boston, MA: South End Press.

Hill, J. 1971. *Personalized education Programs: Utilizing Cognitive Style Mapping.* Bloomfield Hills, MI: Oakland Community College.

Hodgkinson, H. L. 1992. *A Demographic Look at Tomorrow.* Washington, DC: Institute for Educational Leadership.

Hoffman, N. 1981. *Woman's "True" Profession: Voices from the History of Teaching.* Old Westbury, NY: The Feminist Press.

Hoge, R. D. 1988. "Issues in the Definition and Measurement of the Giftedness Construct," *Educational Researcher,* 17(7):12–16.

Hooks, B. 1993. "Transformative Pedagogy and Multiculturalism," in *Freedom's Plow: Teaching in the Multicultural Classroom,* T. Perry and J. W. Fraser, eds., New York, NY: Routledge, pp. 91–97.

Howe, F. 1984. *Myths of Coeducation.* Bloomington, IN: Indiana University Press.

Hunsaker, S. "Instrument Use in the Identification of Gifted and Talented Children," paper presented at *The Meeting of the Jacob K. Javitz Gifted and Talented Education Program Grant Recipients,* Washington, DC, 1991 (unpublished).

Hutchings, P. 1989. *Behind Outcomes: Contexts and Questions for Assessment.* Washington, DC: AAHE.

Hutchings, P. 1990. "Learning over Time: Portfolio Assessment," *AAHE Bulletin,* 42(8):6–8.

Hutchinson, G. E. and B. Johnson. 1993–1994. "Teaching as a Career: Examining High School Students' Perspectives," *Action in Teacher Education,* XV(4):61–67.

Hyde, J. S. 1993. "Gender Differences," talk presented at *The American Psychological Association,* Toronto, Canada.

Jacobs, J. E. 1991. "Influence of Gender Stereotypes on Parent and Child Mathematics Attitudes," *Journal of Educational Psychology,* 83(4):518–527.

Jaeger, R. M. 1991. "Legislative Perspectives on Statewide Testing: Goals, Hopes and Desires," *Phi Delta Kappan,* 73(3):239–242.

Jaggar, A. 1983. *Feminist Politics and Human Nature.* New Jersey: Rowan and Allanheld.

Jalali, F. 1989. "A Cross Cultural Comparative Analysis of Learning Styles and Field Dependence/Independence Characteristics of Selected Fourth-, Fifth-, and Sixth-Grade Students of Afro, Chinese, Greek and Mexican Heritage," Ph.D. diss., St. John's University.

Jones, E. H. and X. P. Montenegro. 1990. *Women and Minorities in School Administration: Facts and Figures, 1989–1990.* Washington, DC: American Association of School Administrators, Office of Minority Affairs.

Kahle, J. B., L. H. Parker, L. J. Rennie and D. Riley. 1993. "Gender Differences in Science Education: Building a Model," *Educational Psychologist,* 28(4): 379–404.

Kamin, L. 1974. *The Science and Politics of IQ.* Potomac, MD: Erlbaum Associates.

Kanter, R. M. 1977. *Men and Women of the Corporation.* New York, NY: Basic Books.

Kaplan, R. M. and D. P. Saccuzzo. 1989. *Psychological Testing.* Pacific Grove, CA: Brooks/Cole.

Keefe, J. W. and B. G. Ferrell. 1990. "Developing a Defensible Learning Style Paradigm," *Educational Leadership,* 48(2):57–61.

Keefe, J. W. and M. L. Languis. "Operational Definitions," paper presented to *The NASSP Learning Styles Task Force,* Reston, Virginia, 1983.

Keefe, J. W. and J. S. Monk. 1986. *Learning Style Profile Examiner's Manual.* Reston, VA: National Association of Secondary School Principals.

Keefe, J., M. Languis, C. Letteri and R. Dunn. 1986. *Learning Style Profile.* Reston, VA: National Association of Secondary School Principals.

Kennedy, M. M. 1992. "Teachers Learn Self-Knowledge from Experience," *Association of Teacher Educators Newsletter,* 26(2):5.

Kimmel, M. S., ed. 1987. *Changing Men: New Directions in Research on Men and Masculinity.* Newbury Park, CA: Sage.

King, J. 1991. "Unfinished Business: Black Student Alienation and Black Teachers' Emancipatory Pedagogy," in *Readings on Equal Education,* M. Foster, ed., New York, NY: AMS Press, pp. 245–271.

King, J. E. 1994. "The Purpose of Schooling for African American Children: Including Cultural Knowledge," in *Teaching Diverse Populations,* E. R. Hollins, J. E. King and W. C. Hayman, eds., Albany, NY: State University of New York, pp. 25–60.

Kirby, J. R. 1988. "Style, Strategy, and Skill in Reading," in *Learning Strategies and Learning Styles,* R. R. Schmeck, ed., New York, NY: Plenum Press, pp. 229–274.

Klein, S., ed. 1985. *Handbook for Achieving Sex Equity through Education.* Baltimore, MD: Johns Hopkins Press.

Knight, C. B. "Effects of Learning Style Accommodation on Achievement of Second Graders," paper presented at *The Meeting of the Mid-South Educational Research Association,* New Orleans, LA, 1990 (unpublished).

Kohl, H. R. 1984. *Growing Minds: On Becoming a Teacher.* New York, NY: Harper and Row.

Kohlberg, L. 1981. *Essays on Moral Development: Vol. 1. The Psychology of Moral Development.* San Francisco, CA: Harper and Row.

Kohlberg, L. 1984. *Essays on Moral Development: Vol. 2. The Psychology of Moral Development.* San Francisco, CA: Harper and Row.

Komarovsky, M. 1950. "Functional Analysis of Sex Roles," *American Sociological Review,* 15:508–516.

Kornhaber, M., M. Krechevsky and H. Gardner. 1990. "Engaging Intelligence," *Educational Psychologist,* 25(3, 4): 177–199.

Kozol, J. 1991. *Savage Inequalities: Children in America's Schools.* New York, NY: Crown Publishers.

Ladson-Billings, G. 1991. "Returning to the Source: Implications for Educating Teachers of Black Students," in *Into Schools and Schooling,* M. Foster, ed., New York, NY: AMS Press, pp. 227–243.

Lankshear, C. and P. L. McLaren, eds. 1993. *Critical Literacy: Politics, Praxis, and the Postmodern.* Albany, NY: State University of New York Press.

Lareau, A. 1987. "Social Class Differences in Family-School Relationships: The Importance of Cultural Capital," *Sociology of Education,* 60(2):73–85.

Larry, P. vs. *Wilson Riles.* 1979. NCO-71-2270 RFP. U.S. District Court for Northern District of California.

Lather, P. 1991. *Getting Smart: Feminist Research and Pedagogy with/in the Postmodern.* New York, NY: Routledge.

Lerner, J. 1981. *Learning Disabilities: Theories, Diagnosis, and Teaching Strategies.* Boston, MA: Houghton Mifflin.

LeVine, R. and M. White. 1986. *Human Conditions: The Cultural Basis of Educational Development.* New York, NY: Routledge & Kegan Paul.

Lewin, K. 1952. "Group Decisions and Social Change," in *Readings in Social Psychology,* G. E. Swanson, T. M. Newcomb and F. E. Hartley, eds., New York, NY: Holt.

Lightfoot, S. L. 1983. *The Good High School.* New York, NY: Basic Books.

Lightfoot, S. L. 1988. *Balm in Gilead: Journey of a Healer.* Reading, MA: Addison-Wesley.

Lorde, A. 1984. *Sister Outsider.* New York, NY: Crossing Press.

Lubeck, S. 1985. *Sandbox Society: Early Education in Black and White America—A Comparative Ethnography.* London, England: The Falmer Press.

Maccoby, R. R. 1966. *The Development of Sex Differences.* Stanford, CT: Stanford University Press.

Maccoby, E. E. and C. N. Jacklin. 1974. *The Psychology of Sex Differences.* Palo Alto, CA: Stanford University Press.

MacDonald, B. 1973. "Briefing Decision Makers," in *School Evaluation: The Politics and Process,* E. R. House, ed., Berkeley, CA: McCutchan, pp. 174–187.

Macias, R. F. 1989. *The National Need for Bilingual Teachers.* Claremont, CA: Tomas Rivera Center.

MacLeod, J. 1987. *Ain't No Makin' It: Leveled Aspirations in a Low-Income Neighborhood.* Boulder, CO: Westview.

Madaus, G. F. 1993. "A National Testing System: Manna from Above? An Historical/Technological Perspective," *Educational Assessment,* 1(1):9–26.

Marshall, C. 1985. "From Culturally Defined to Self-Defined Career Stages of Women Administrators," *The Journal of Educational Thought,* 19(2):134–147.

McCarthy, C. and M. W. Apple. 1988. "Race, Class and Gender in American Educational Research: Toward a Nonsynchronous Parallelist Position," in *Class, Race and Gender in American Education,* L. Weiss, ed., Albany, NY: SUNY Press.

McIntosh, P. 1984. *Interactive Phases of Curricular Revision: A Feminist Perspective.* Wellesley, MA: Wellesley College Center for Research on Women.

McLaren, P. 1989. *Life in Schools.* New York, NY: Longman.

McLaren, P. and P. Leonard, eds. 1993. *Paulo Freire: A Critical Encounter.* London, England: Routledge.

McLaughlin, M. W. 1991. "Test-Based Accountability as a Reform Strategy," *Phi Delta Kappan,* 73(3):248–250.

McNeil, L. M. 1986. *Contradictions of Control: School Structure and School Knowledge.* London, England: Routledge & Kegan Paul.

McTighe, C. M., ed. 1992. *The Courage to Question: Women's Studies and Student Learning.* Washington, DC: Association of American Colleges.

Mead, M., T. G. Dobzhensky and D. B. Light, eds. 1968. *Science and the Concept of Race.* New York, NY: Columbia University Press.

Melton, G. 1989. "Public Policy and Private Prejudice: Psychology and Law on Gay Rights," *American Psychologist,* 44(6):933–940.

Mensh, E. and H. Mensh. 1991. *The IQ Mythology.* Carbondale, IL: Southern Illinois Press,

Michaels, S. 1981. " 'Sharing Time': Children's Narrative Styles and Differential Access to Literacy," *Language in Society,* 10:423–442.

Mickelson, R. 1990. "The Attitude-Achievement Paradox among Black Adolescents," *Sociology of Education,* 63:44–61.

Miller, J. 1990. *Creating Spaces and Finding Voices: Teachers Collaborating for Empowerment.* Albany, NY: State University of New York.

Mitchell, J. T. 1990. "In Search of Organizational Culture: A Case Study of an Excellent High School," *DAI,* 50:3124A.

Mohr, M. and M. Maclean. 1987. *Working Together: A Guide for Teacher-Researchers.* Urbana, IL: National Council of English Teachers.

Montagu, A. 1974. *Man's Most Dangerous Myth: The Fallacy of Race.* New York, NY: Oxford University Press.

Munoz, C., Jr. 1989. *Youth, Identity and Power.* London, England: Verso.

Murphy, S. and M. A. Smith. 1990. "Talking about Portfolios," *The Quarterly of the National Writing Project and the Center for the Study of Writing,* 12(1):1–3.

Murrell, P. C. 1991. "What Is Missing in the Preparation of Minority Teachers?" in *Into Schools and Schooling,* M. Foster, ed., New York, NY: AMS Press, pp. 205–225.

NASSP National Task Force. 1983. "National Task Force Defines Learning Style Operationally and Conceptually," *Learning Styles Network Newsletter,* 4(2):1.

National Center for Education Statistics. 1989. *Selected Characteristics of Public School Teachers: Spring 1961 to Spring 1986.* Washington, DC: NCES.

National Joint Committee on Learning Disabilities (NJCLD). 1988. Letter to NJCLD member organizations.

National Policy Board for Educational Administration. 1989. *Improving the Preparation of School Administrators.* Charlotteville, VA: University of Virginia.

National Science Foundation. 1990. *Women and Minorities in Science and Engineering.* Washington, DC: Author.

New York Times. June 14, 1992. Vol. CXLI, #48997.

Noddings, N. 1984. *Caring: A Feminine Approach to Ethics and Moral Education.* Berkeley, CA: University of California Press.

Noddings, N. 1991. "Stories in Dialogue: Caring and Interpersonal Reasoning," in *Stories Lives Tell: Narrative and Dialogue in Education,* New York, NY: Teachers College Press, pp. 157–170.

Noddings, N. 1992. *The Challenge to Care in Schools: An Alternative Approach to Education.* New York, NY: Teachers College Press.

Nordin, V. 1989. "*GRC* v. *Georgetown*: Autonomy and Nondiscrimination," *Thought and Action,* 5(2):32–47.

Oakes, J. 1990. *Multiplying Inequities: The Effects of Race, Social Class and Tracking on Opportunities to Learn Mathematics and Science.* Santa Monica, CA: Rand Corporation.

Ogbu, J. 1987a. *Minority Education and Caste: The American System in Cross-Cultural Perspective.* New York, NY: Academic Press.

Ogbu, J. 1987b. "Variability in Minority School Performance: A Problem in Search of an Explanation," *Anthropology and Education Quarterly,* 18(4):312–334.

Ortiz, F. I. and C. Marshall. 1988. "Women in Educational Administration," in *Handbook of Research on Educational Administration,* N. J. Bryan, ed., New York, NY: Longman.

Ovando, C. J. 1993. "Language Diversity and Education," in *Multicultural Education: Issues and Perspectives.* Second edition. Boston, MA: Allyn and Bacon.

Parker, L. and S. Hood. "Perceptions of Minority Teacher Education Students at Two Holmes Group Institutions: Diversity, Equity, and Social Justice," paper presented at *The American Educational Research Association Annual Meeting,* Chicago, IL, 1991 (unpublished).

Parker, L. and J. P. Shapiro. 1993. "The Context of Educational Administration and Social Class," in *Educational Administration in a Pluralistic Society,* C. A. Capper, ed., Albany, NY: State University of New York Press.

Pavan, B. N. 1985. "Certified But Not Hired: Women Administrators in Pennsylvania," paper presented at *The Research on Women in Education Conference,* Boston. (ERIC Documentation Reproduction Service No. ED 263 689).

Pearl, A. 1991. "Democratic Education: Myth or Reality," in *Chicano School Failure and Success,* R. Valencia, ed., New York, NY: Falmer Press, pp. 101–118.

Perry, I. 1988. "A Black Student's Reflection on Public and Private Schools," *Harvard Educational Review,* 58:332–336.

Philadephia Inquirer. "A Diverse U.S. Seen in the Census," May 30, 1992, pp. A1, A7.

Philadelphia Inquirer. "Female Students Cheated by National Merit Test," June 6, 1994, p. A11.

Philadelphia Citizens for Children and Youth. 1989. *The Health Status of Philadelphia's Children.* Philadelphia, PA.

Piaget, J. 1952. *The Language and Thought of the Child.* London, England: Routledge & Kegan Paul.

Pleck, J. H. 1981. *The Myth of Masculinity.* Cambridge, MA: MIT Press.

Popkewitz, T. S. 1992. "Culture, Pedagogy, and Power," in *What Schools Can Do: Critical Pedagogy and Practice*, K. Weiler and C. Mitchell, eds., Albany, NY: State University of New York Press, pp. 133–148.

Purpel, D. E. 1989. *The Moral and Spiritual Crisis in Education: A Curriculum for Justice and Compassion in Education.* Granby, MA: Bergin & Garvey.

Reich, R. B. 1992. *The Work of Nations: Preparing Ourselves for 21st Century Capitalism.* New York, NY: Vintage Books.

Reis, S. M. 1989. "Reflections on Policy Affecting the Education of Gifted and Talented Students: Past and Future Perspectives," *American Psychologist,* 44(2):399–408.

Renzulli, J. S. 1986. "The Three-Ring Conception of Giftedness: A Developmental Model for Creative Productivity," in *Conceptions of Giftedness,* R. J. Sternberg and J. E. Davidson, eds., Cambridge, MA: Cambridge University Press, pp. 53–92.

Renzulli, J. S. and S. M. Reis. 1991. "The Reform Movement and the Quiet Crisis in Gifted Education," *Gifted Child Quarterly,* 35(1):26–35.

Reynolds, M. C. 1988. "Students with Special Needs," in *A Knowledge Base for Teachers,* M. C. Reynolds, ed., New York, NY: Pergamon Press.

Rich, A. 1979. *On Lies, Secrets, and silence: Selected Prose 1966–1978.* New York, NY: W. W. Norton.

Rich, A. 1983. "Compulsory Heterosexuality and Lesbian Existence," in *The SIGNS Reader: Women, Gender and Scholarship,* E. Abel and E. K. Abel, eds., Chicago, IL: The University of Chicago Press, pp. 139–168.

Richardson, L. and V. Taylor, eds. 1993. *Feminist Frontiers III.* New York, NY: McGraw-Hill.

Robins, P. M. 1992. "A Comparison of Behavioral and Attentional Functioning in Children as Hyperactive or Learning-Disabled," *Journal of Abnormal Child Psychology,* 20(1):65–82.

Robinson, C. J. 1983. *Black Marxism: The Making of the Black Radical Tradition.* London, England: Zed Press.

Rofes, E. 1989. "Opening up the Classroom Closet: Responding to the Educational Needs of Gay and Lesbian Youth," *Harvard Educational Review,* 59(4):444–453.

Rorty, R. 1979. *Philosophy and the Mirror of Nature.* Princeton, NJ: Princeton University Press.

Rose, P. I. 1990. *They and We: Racial and Ethnic Relations in the United States.* New York, NY: Random House.

Rosenshine, B. and R. Stevens. 1986. "Teaching Functions," in *Handbook of Research on Teaching.* Third edition, M. C. Wittrock, ed., Washington, DC: American Educational Research Association, pp. 376–391.

Ross, E. W., J. W. Cornett and G. McCutcheon, eds. 1992. *Teacher Personal Theorizing: Connecting Curriculum Practice, Theory, and Research.* Albany, NY: State University of New York.

Rosser, P. 1989. *The SAT Gender Gap.* Washington, DC: Center for Women's Policy Studies.

Rowan, J. 1987. *The Horned God.* New York, NY: Routledge & Kegan Paul.

Rowland v. *Mad River Local School District Montgomery County.* 1985. 730 F. 2d 444, 445-446 (6th Cir. 1984), Cert. denied, 470 U.S. 1009, 105 S. Ct. 1373, 84 L. Ed. 2d. 393 [23 Ed. Law Rep. 26].

Russo, V. 1981. *The Celluloid Closet: Homosexuality in the Movies.* New York, NY: Harper & Row.

Rutter, M. 1989. "Attention Deficit Disorder/Hyperkinetic Syndrome: Conceptual and Research Issues Regarding Diagnosis and Classification," in *Attention Deficit Disorder: Clinical and Basic Research,* T. Sagvolden and T. Archer, eds., Hillsdale, NJ: Erlbaum, pp. 1–24.

Ryan, K. 1970. *Don't Smile until Christmas: Accounts of the First Year of Teaching.* Chicago, IL: University of Chicago Press.

Sabatay, V. 1991. "The Stranger's Story: Who Calls and Who Answers?" in *Stories Lives Tell: Narrative and Dialogue in Education,* C. Witherell and N. Noddings, eds., New York, NY: Teacher College Press, pp. 36–152.

Sadker, M. and D. Sadker. 1982. *Sex Equity Handbook for Schools.* New York, NY: Longman.

Sadker, M. and D. Sadker. 1994. *Failing at Fairness: How America's Schools Cheat Girls.* New York, NY: Scribners.

Sadker, M., D. Sadker and S. Klein. 1991. "The Issue of Gender in Elementary and Secondary Education," G. Grant, ed., in *Review of Research in Education,* 17:269–334.

Samuda, R. 1975. *Psychological Testing of American Minorities: Issues and Consequences.* New York, NY: Dodd, Mead and Co.

Sarason, S. 1985. *Schooling in America: Scapegoat and Salvation.* New York, NY: The Free Press.

Schiff, M. and R. Lewontin. 1986. *Education and Class: The Irrelevance of IQ Genetic Studies.* Oxford, England: Oxford University Press.

Schmitz, B. and A. S. Willliams. 1983. *Sourcebook for Integrating the Study of Women into the Curriculum.* Bozeman, MT: Northwest Women's Studies Association.

Schniedewind, N. and F. Maher, eds. 1987. "Special Feature: Feminist Pedagogy," *Women's Studies Quarterly,* 15(3,4):6–124.

Schubert, W. H. 1992. "Personal Theorizing about Teacher Personal Theorizing," in *Teacher Personal Theorizing: Connecting Curriculum Practice, Theory, and Research,* E. W. Ross, J. W. Cornett and G. McCutcheon, eds., Albany, NY: State University of New York Press, pp. 257–272.

Schuhmann, A. M. 1992. "Learning to Teach Hispanic Students," in *Diversity in Teacher Education: New Expectations,* M. E. Dilworth, ed., San Francisco, CA: Jossey-Bass.

Schuster, M. R. and S. R. Van Dyne, eds. 1985. *Women's Place in the Academy: Transforming the Liberal Arts Curriculum.* Totowa, NJ: Roman & Allanheld.

Sears, J. 1989. "The Impact of Gender and Race on Growing up Lesbian and Gay in the South," *National Women's Studies Association Journal,* 1(3):422–457.

Sears, J. 1991. *Growing up Gay in the South: Race, Gender, and Journeys of the Spirit.* New York, NY: Haworth Press.

Sears, J. 1992. "The Impact of Culture and Ideology on the Construction of Gender and Sexual Identities: Developing a Critically-Based Sexuality Curriculum," in *Sexuality and the Curriculum,* J. Sears, ed., New York, NY: Teachers College Press, pp. 169–189.

Sears, J. 1993. "Responding to the Sexual Diversity of Faculty and Students: Sexual Praxis and the Critical Reflective Administrator," in *Educational Administration in a Pluralistic Society,* C. A. Capper, ed., Albany, NY: State University of New York Press, pp. 110–172.

Sewell, T. E. 1979. "Intelligence and Learning Tasks as Predictors of Scholastics Achievement in Black and White First Grade Children," *Journal of School Psychology,* 17:325–332.

Sewell, T. E. 1987. "Dynamic Assessment as a Non-Discrimatory Procedure," in C. Lidz, ed., *Dynamic Assessment: Foundations and Fundamentals.* NY: Guilford Publications.

Sewell, T. E. 1988. "Intellectual Assessment of At-risk Students: Classification vs. Instructional Goals," in *At-Risk Students and Thinking: Perspectives from Research,* B. Presseisen, ed., Philadelphia, PA: National Educational Association/Research for Better Schools.

Sewell, T. E. 1990. "Testing African American Children: Have Ideological Beliefs Masked the Education Benefits?" *The State of Black Philadelphia,* 9:29–36.

Sewell, T. E., J. P. DuCette and J. P. Shapiro. 1991. "Cultural Diversity and Educational Assessment," paper presented at *The American Psychological Association Annual Conference,* San Francisco, CA.

Shade, B. J. 1982. "African-American Cognitive Style: A Variable in School Success?" *Review of Educational Research,* 52(2):219–244.

Shade, B. J. 1986. "Is There an Afro-American Cognitive Style?" *Journal of Black Psychology,* 13:13–16.

Shade, B. J. 1989. *Culture and Learning Style within the Afro-American Community.* New York, NY: Charles Stone Publishing.

Shakeshaft, C. 1987. *Women in Educational Administration.* Newbury Park, CA: Sage.

Shapiro, J. P. 1987. "Women in Education: At Risk or Prepared?" *The Educational Forum,* 51:167–183.

Shapiro, J. P. 1990. "Non-Feminist and Feminist Students at Risk: The Use of Case Study Analysis while Transforming the Postsecondary Curriculum," *Women's Studies International Forum,* 13(4):553–564.

Shapiro, J. P. 1992. "What Is Feminist Assessment?" in *Students at the Center: Feminist Assessment,* C. McTighe Musil, ed., Washington, DC: Association of American Colleges.

Shapiro, J. P., J. P. DuCette and T. E. Sewell. 1993. "A Critique of Approaches for Reframing the Paradox between the Multicultural Curriculum and Accountability," paper presented at *The American Educational Research Association Annual Meeting,* Atlanta, GA.

Shapiro, J. P., C. Parssinen and S. Brown. 1992. "Teacher-Scholars: An Action Research Study of a Collaborative Feminist Scholarship Colloquium between Schools and Universities," *Teaching and Teacher Education,* 8(1):91–104.

Shapiro, J. P. and C. Smith-Rosenberg. 1989. "The 'Other Voices' in Contemporary Ethical Dilemmas: The Value of the New Scholarship on Women in the Teaching of Ethics," *Women's Studies International Forum,* 12(6):199–211.

Shapiro, S. 1990. *Between Capitalism and Democracy: Educational Policy and the Crisis of the Welfare State.* New York, NY: Bergin & Garvey.

Shephard, L. A. 1991. "Will National Tests Improve Student Learning?" *Phi Delta Kappan,* 73(3):232–238.

Shor, I. 1980. *Critical Teaching and Everyday Life.* Boston, MA: South End Press.

Shrewsbury, C. M. 1987. "What Is Feminist Pedagogy?" *Women's Studies Quarterly,* 15(3,4):6–14.

Silberman, A. 1989. *Growing up Writing.* New York, NY: Time Book.

Simons, H. 1971. "Innovation and the Case Study of School," *Cambridge Journal of Education,* 3:118–123.

Slavin, R. E. and N. A. Madden. 1989. "A Meta-Analysis of the Effect of Enhanced Instruction: Cues, Participation, Reinforcement, Feedback, and Correctives on Motor Skill Learning," *Journal of Research and Development in Education,* 22(3):53–64.

Sleeter, C. E., ed. 1991. *Empowerment through Multicultural Education.* Albany, NY: State University of New York Press.

Sleeter, C. E. 1992a. *Keepers of the American Dream: A Study of Staff Development and Multicultural Education.* London, England: Falmer Press.

Sleeter, C. E. 1992b. "Resisting Racial Awareness: How Teachers Understand the Social Order from Their Racial, Gender, and Social Class Locations," *Educational Foundations,* 6(2):7–32.

Sleeter, C. E. and C. A. Grant. 1988. *Making Choices for Multicultural Education: Five Approaches to Race, Class and Gender.* New York, NY: Macmillan.

Smith, M. B. 1994. "Selfhood at Risk: Postmodern Perils and the Perils of Postmodernism," *American Psychologist,* 49(5):405–411.

Smith-Rosenberg, C. C. 1983. "Female World of Love and Ritual: Relations between Women in Nineteenth-Century America," in *The SIGNS Reader: Women, Gender and Scholarship,* E. Abel and E. K. Abel, eds., Chicago, IL: The University of Chicago Press, pp. 27–56.

Spanier, B., A. Bloom and D. Boroviak, eds. 1986. *Women's Studies in the United States: A Report to the Ford Foundation.* New York, NY: Ford Foundation.

Spearman, C. 1927. *The Abilities of Man.* New York, NY: Macmillan.

Spender, D. 1982. *Invisible Women: The Schooling Scandal.* London, England: Writers and Readers.

Stainback, W. and S. Stainback. 1990. "Inclusive Schooling," in *Support Networks for Inclusive Schooling,* W. Stainback and S. Stainback, eds., Baltimore, MD: Paul H. Brookes, pp. 3–23.

Stake, R. E. 1991. "The Teacher, Standardized Testing, and Prospects of Revolution," *Phi Delta Kappan,* 73(3):243–247.

Stanworth, M. 1983. *Gender and Schooling: A Study of Sexual Division in the Classroom.* London, England: Hutchinson.

Starratt, R. J. 1994. *Building and Ethical School: A Practical Response to the Moral Crisis in Schools.* London, England: The Falmer Press.

Steele, C. M. 1992. "Race and the Schooling of Black Americans," *The Atlantic,* 269(4):68–78.

Steele, G. E. 1986. "An Investigation of the Relationship between Students' Interests and the Curricular Practices of an Alternative High School through the Perspective of Jung's Theory of Psychological Types," *Dissertation Abstracts International,* 47:3616–A.

Stefkovich, J. A. and J. P. Shapiro. 1995. "Personal and Professional Ethics for Educational Administrators: Nontraditional and Pedagogical Implications," *Review Journal of Philosophy and Social Science,* 20(1&2):157–186.

Steinberg, L., S. M. Dornbusch and B. B. Brown. 1992. "Ethnic Differences in

Adolescent Achievement: An Ecological Perspective," *American Psychologist,* 46(6):723–729.

Steinhaurer, J. 1994. "The Principles of Success," *The New York Times,* Vol. CXLIII, Section 4A, pp. 36–37.

Stenhouse, L. 1975. *Introduction to Curriculum Research and Development.* London, England: Heinemann.

Stenhouse, L. 1985. *Research as a Basis for Teaching.* London, England: Heinemann.

Sternberg, R. 1988. "Mental Self-Government: A Theory of Intellectual Styles and Their Development," *Human Development,* 31:197–224.

Sternberg, R. 1990. *Wisdom: Its Nature, Origins, and Development.* New York, NY: Cambridge University Press.

Sternberg, R. 1992. "Ability Tests, Measurement, and Markets," *Journal of Educational Psychology,* 84(2):134–140.

Sternberg, R. J. and J. E. Davidson, eds. 1986. *Conceptions of Giftedness.* Cambridge, MA: Cambridge University Press, pp. 53–92.

Stiles, R. H. 1985. "Learning Style Preferences for Design and Their Relationship to Standardized Test Results," *Dissertation Abstracts International,* 43(01):68A.

Strike, K. A., E. J. Haller and J. F. Soltis. 1988. *The Ethics of School Administration.* New York, NY: The Teachers College Press.

Strober, M. H. and D. Tyack. 1980. "Why Do Women Teach and Men Manage? A Report on Research on Schools," *SIGNS,* 5:497.

Styles, E. J. 1988. *SEED Project Newsletter.* Wellesley, MA: Wellesley College Center for Research on Women.

Suzuki, B. H. 1984. "Curriculum Transformation for Multicultural Education," *Education and Urban Society,* 16:294–322.

Tabor, M. 1992. "For Gay High-School Seniors, Nightmare Is Almost Over," *New York Times,* June 14, Vol. CXLI (48997), pp. 40, 44.

Tafoya, T. 1994. "Understanding and Serving American Indian Students," presented at *The Multicultural Infusion Network Institute,* San Diego, CA, June 10, 1994.

Tannenbaum, R. 1982. "An Investigation of the Relationships between Selected Instructional Techniques and Identified Field Dependent and Field Independent Cognitive Styles as Evidenced among High School Students Enrolled in Studies of Nutrition," *Dissertation Abstracts International,* 43(01):68A.

Terman, L. 1916. *The Measurements of Intelligence.* Boston, MA: Houghton Mifflin.

Tetreault, M. K. T. 1989. "Integrating Content about Women and Gender into the Curriculum," in *Multicultural Education: Issues and Perspectives.* Boston, MA: Allyn and Bacon, pp. 124–144.

Tetreault, M. K. and P. Schmuck. 1985. "Equity, Educational Reform, and Gender," *Issues in Education,* 3(1):45–67.

Tharpe, R. G. 1989. "Psychocultural Variables and k Constants: Effects on Teaching and Learning in Schools," *American Psychologist,* 44:349–359.

Thurstone, L. 1938. *Primary Mental Abilities.* Chicago, IL: University of Chicago Press.

Tittle, C. K. 1991. "Testing in Educational Placement: Issues and Evidence," in *Placing Children in Special Education: A Strategy for Equity,* K. Heller, W. Holtzman and S. Messick, eds., Washington, DC: National Academy Press.

Torrey, J. E. 1983. "Black Children's Knowledge of Standard English," *American Educational Research Journal,* 20(4):627.

Trent, W. T. 1988. "Class, Culture, and Schooling: Reframing the Questions," a presentation to the faculty of the University of Illinois at the Wingspread Conference Center, Racine, WI.

Trueba, H. 1988. "Culturally Based Explanations of Minority Students' Academic Achievement," *Anthropology and Education Quarterly,* 19:270–287.

U.S. Department of Education. 1990. *Current Population Reports.* Washington, DC: Government Printing Office.

van den Berghe, P. L., ed. 1978. *Race and Racism: A Comparative Perspective.* New York, NY: John Wiley.

Viadero, D. 1994. "Teaching to the Test," *Education Week,* XIII(39):21–25.

Walberg, H. J. 1986. "Synthesis of Research on Teaching," in *Handbook of Research on Teaching.* Third edition, M. C. Wittrock, ed., Washington, DC: American Educational Research Association.

Walter, J. and H. Gardner. 1986. "The Theory of Multiple Intelligences: Same Issues and Answers," in *Practical Intelligence,* R. Sternberg and R. Wagner, eds., Cambridge, MA: Cambridge University Press.

Walters, J. and H. Gardner. 1991. *Portfolios of Student Projects: Continuing Research on a New Approach to Assessment* (Project Zero Report to the Lilly Endowment). Cambridge, MA: Harvard Graduate School of Education.

Walters, J. and S. Seidel. 1991. *The Design of Portfolios for Authentic Student Assessment* (Tech. Rep., Project Zero). Cambridge, MA: Harvard Graduate School of Education.

Walters, J., S. Seidel and H. Gardner. 1994. "Children as Reflective Practitioners: Bringing Metacognition to the Classroom," in *Mindfulness: Creating Powerful Thinkers,* C. Collins and J. Mangieri, eds., Fort Worth, TX: Harcourt, Brace, and Janovich.

Wang, M. C., G. D. Haertel and H. J. Walberg. 1993. "Toward a Knowledge Base for School Learning," *Review of Educational Research,* 63(3):249–294.

Weiler, K. and C. Mitchell, eds. 1992. *What Schools Can Do: Critical Pedagogy and Practice.* Albany, NY: State University of New York Press.

Weis, L. 1990. *Working Class without Work. High School Students in a De-Industrializing Economy.* London, England: Routledge & Kegan Paul.

Weisner, T. S., R. Gallimore and C. Jordan. 1988. "Unpacking Cultural Effects on Classroom Learning. Native Hawaiian Peer Assistance and Child-Generated Activity," *Anthropology and Educational Quarterly,* 19(4):327–353.

Weiss, L. and M. Fine, eds. 1993. *Beyond Silenced Voices: Class, Race, and Gender in United States Schools.* Albany, NY: State University of New York Press.

Welch, S. D. 1985. *Communities of Resistance and Solidarity: A Feminist Theology of Liberation.* Maryknoll, NY: Orbis Books.

Welch, S. D. 1991. "An Ethic of Solidarity and Difference," in *Postmodernism, Feminism, and Cultural Politics: Redrawing Educational Boundaries,* H. A. Giroux, ed., Albany, NY: State University of New York, pp. 83–99.

Wexler, P. 1982. "Structure, Text, and Subject: A Critical Sociology of School Knowledge," in *Cultural and Economic Reproduction in Education,* M. W. Apple, ed., London, England: Routledge & Kegan Paul, pp. 275–303.

Wiggins, G. 1989. "A True Test: Towards a More Authentic and Equitable Assessment," *Phi Delta Kappan,*70:703–713.

Wiggins, G. 1991. "Standards, Not Standardization: Evoking Quality Student Work," *Educational Leadership,* 48(5)18–25.

Wiggins, G. P. 1993. *Assessing Student Performance: Exploring the Purpose and Limits of Testing.* San Francisco, CA: Jossey-Bass.

Williams, J. E. and S. M. Bennett. 1975. "The Definition of Sex Stereotyping via the Adjective Check List," *Sex Roles,* 1:327–337.

Willis, P. 1977. *Learning to Labor.* Westmead, Farnborough Hants, England: Saxon House, Teakfield Limited.

Winner, F. D. 1983. *Genetic Basis of Society.* Dunedin, FL: Shakespeare Publishing Co.

Witherell, C. and N. Noddings, eds. 1991. *Stories Lives Tell: Narrative and Dialogue in Education.* New York, NY: Teachers College Press.

Witken, H. A., R. B. Dyk, H. F. Faterson, D. R. Goodenough and S. A. Karp. 1974. *Psychological Differentiation: Studies of Development.* Potomac, MD: Lawrence Erlbaum Associates.

Wittgenstein, L. 1968. *Philosophical Investigations.* (G. E. M. Anscombe, Trans). New York, NY: Macmillan.

Wong-Fillmore, L. 1991. "Second-Language Learning in Children: A Model of Language Learning in Social Context," in *Language Processing in Bilingual Children,* E. Bialystok, ed., Cambridge, England: Cambridge University Press, pp. 49–69.

Wong-Fillmore, L. 1994. "Strategies for Second Language Acquisition," presentation at *The Multicultural Infusion Center Institute,* San Diego, CA: San Diego State University.

Worthen, B. 1991. "Critical Issues That Will Determine the Future of Alternative Assessment," *Phi Delta Kappan,* 74(6).

Yancey, L., I. Goldstein and D. Webb. 1987. *The Ecology of Health and Educational Outcomes: An Analysis of Philadelphia Public Elementary Schools,* Philadelphia, PA: Temple University, Institute of Public Policy.

Yesseldyke, J. E. and B. Algozzine. 1983. "LD or Not LD: That's Not the Question," *Journal of Learning Disabilities,* 16(1):29–31.

Zaretsky, E. 1976. *Capitalism, the Family, and Personal Life.* New York, NY: Harper and Row.

Zessoules, R. and G. Gardner. 1991. "Authentic Assessment: Beyond the Buzzword and into the Classroom," in *Expanding Student Assessment,* V. Perrone, ed., Washington, DC: Association for Supervision and Curriculum Development.

INDEX